TEACHING CHILDREN GYMNASTICS

Becoming a Master Teacher

PETER H. WERNER, PED

University of South Carolina, Columbia

Human Kinetics

Library of Congress Cataloging-in-Publication Data

Werner, Peter H.
  Teaching children gymnastics : becoming a master teacher / Peter
Werner.
    p.   cm.
  Includes bibliographical references.
  ISBN 0-87322-477-9
  1. Gymnastics for children--Coaching.   I. Title.
GV464.5.W47   1994
796.44--dc20   93-21409
                                                         CIP

ISBN: 0-87322-477-9

Acquisitions Editor: Scott Wikgren
Series Editor: George Graham, PhD
AMTP Content Editor: Christine Hopple
Developmental Editor: Julia Anderson
Assistant Editors: Dawn Roselund and Jacqueline Blakley
Copyeditor: Anne Mischakoff-Heiles
Proofreader: Anne Byler
Production Director: Ernie Noa
Typesetting and Text Layout: Sandra Meier
Illustration Coordinators: Tara Welsch and Kris Slamans
Text Designer: Keith Blomberg
Cover Designer: Jody Boles
Photographer (cover): Bob Veltri
Cover Models: Andrew Baffi, Nick Baffi, Emily Carstenson, Jennifer Shephard
Illustrators: Mary Yemma Long, Gretchen Walters, Kathy Boudreau-Fuoss
Printer: United Graphics

Printed in the United States of America

10   9   8   7   6   5   4   3   2

Human Kinetics
P.O. Box 5076, Champaign, IL 61825-5076
1-800-747-4457

Canada: Human Kinetics, Box 24040, Windsor, ON N8Y 4Y9
1-800-465-7301 (in Canada only)

Europe: Human Kinetics, P.O. Box IW14, Leeds LS16 6TR, United Kingdom
(44) 1132 781708

Australia: Human Kinetics, 2 Ingrid Street, Clapham 5062, South Australia
(08) 371 3755

New Zealand: Human Kinetics, P.O. Box 105-231, Auckland 1
(09) 523 3462

Contents

Series Preface

In the United States most children spend 6 to 7 years in elementary schools, from Kindergarten through sixth grade. Assume that they participate in instructional physical education classes twice a week for the entire time. Each class is 30 minutes long—a total of 36 hours a year and 216 hours over 6 years. Because of interruptions such as snow days, field trips, school plays, absences, and arriving late to physical education class, the time actually spent in physical education may be closer to 150 hours—perhaps less. Still 150 hours is a substantial amount of time. But what do children learn in that time? What is realistic to expect they might learn?

The answers vary. Some children might learn that physical activity is enjoyable, something they choose to do on their own with friends after school and on weekends. Others might learn that they are not good at sports and search for other ways to spend their leisure time. Others might really like their PE classes and the teacher but, given a choice, prefer to watch television or sit around when they're at home. The 150 hours, hopefully more, that a child spends in physical education classes influence his or her decisions—as a child, and for a lifetime!

What do we expect children to learn in elementary school physical education? Until recently the answer to this question was left solely to the individual teacher or school district. Physical educators across the United States had no universal sense of the outcomes that might accrue from quality programs of physical education. But this changed in 1992, when the National Association for Sport and Physical Education (NASPE)

completed 7 years of work on a document titled *The Physically Educated Person.* This document outlined, for the first time, a nationally developed and endorsed framework for planning and evaluating physical education programs, from preschool through grade 12. This book, and the other volumes in this series, were developed using the outcomes and benchmarks developed by NASPE as a general guide.

As you might imagine, the American Master Teacher Program (AMTP) struggled with how to organize the content. Should there be one book? Several books? Which model should we use to organize the content? Ultimately we chose to develop five books on the following topics: basic movement skills and concepts, games, gymnastics, dance, and fitness concepts. We decided to publish several books instead of just one because it seemed to be the most widely understood approach to organizing the content in physical education. It also provided the opportunity to involve several authors who were recognized for their expertise in their respective areas.

As we were considering possible authors, we made lists of who we thought were the best qualified individuals to write these books. In each instance, we are delighted to say, the author or authors we thought most qualified accepted our invitation to write the book. The books are as follows:

- *Teaching Children Movement Concepts and Skills: Becoming a Master Teacher* by Craig Buschner
- *Teaching Children Dance: Becoming a Master Teacher* by Theresa Purcell

- *Teaching Children Gymnastics: Becoming a Master Teacher* by Peter Werner
- *Teaching Children Games: Becoming a Master Teacher* by David Belka
- *Teaching Children Fitness: Becoming a Master Teacher* by Tom and Laraine Ratliffe

In addition, we want to thank Dr. Paula Ely, principal of Margaret Beeks Elementary School in Blacksburg, VA, for her ongoing support of various aspects of the American Master Teacher Program.

Each book is divided into two parts. The first part contains five chapters, which include a description of the content, an explanation of how it is organized, and most importantly the reasons why the author or authors believe that content is important for children to learn. One problem that has plagued physical education in elementary schools is that programs all too often have lacked an underlying theory or purpose. It seemed that teachers were just trying to entertain the children, rather than to actually teach them. For this reason, we hope you will begin reading this book by carefully reading Part I so that you can better understand the content—and *why* it is important for children to learn.

Part II contains the activities, or learning experiences (LEs). These three chapters contain the actual "stuff" to do with children. It is more than just stuff, however. Part II presents a logical progression of activities designed to lead children toward a heightened understanding and improved competence in the content described in the book. After you read the content described in Part I, you will be better able to envision where the LEs are leading—and the importance of the progression and sequencing of these activities will be clear to you. From the standpoint of the author, and ultimately the children, it would be unfortunate if a teacher completely skipped Part I and then searched Part II for activities that appeared to be the most fun and exciting—and then taught them in a haphazard way without any logical sequencing or order to the program. Children truly enjoy learning! These books are designed to help them do just that; the purpose is not just to keep them busy for a few minutes several times a week.

Finally, it is important to emphasize that *the contents of all five books are important* for the children's physical education. One danger in doing a series of books is that a mistaken impression might be given that a content area can be skipped altogether. This is not the case. Just as it wouldn't make sense for math teachers to skip subtraction or division because they didn't like to "take things away" or "weren't very good at it," it doesn't make sense to skip dance or gymnastics, for example, because a teacher has never had a course in it or isn't confident about teaching it. We realize, however, that many physical education teachers feel less confident about teaching dance or gymnastics; this is the primary reason the books were written—and why the AMTP was founded. It is certainly OK to feel anxious or unconfident about teaching one, or more, of the content areas. It's not OK, however, not to teach them because of these feelings. Many of us have experienced these same feelings, but with experience, work, and support, we have gradually incorporated them into our programs—and done so in ways that are both beneficial and enjoyable for children. This is what we want to help you to do as well. And that's why the books were written and the AMTP was developed.

Each of the five content books also has a companion videotape that provides examples of actual lessons selected from the learning experiences. These consolidated lessons show you how a few LEs might be developed with children. In addition to the videotapes, workshops are available through the American Master Teacher Program to help you gain a better understanding of the content and how it is taught. The authors of the books realize that making the transition from a traditional program to teaching this content is not easy, and yet increasingly teachers are realizing that children deserve more than simply being entertained in the name of physical education. We hope you will find the books worthwhile—and helpful—and that the children you teach will benefit!

George Graham
Cofounder and Director of Curriculum
  and Instruction
American Master Teacher Program

Preface

As a child I was always attracted to gymnastics kinds of activities. In my parochial elementary school, physical education was not offered. Fortunately, I was an active child. I remember swinging and sliding on playgrounds and playing sandlot baseball, football, and youth basketball. When I got to high school, I was excused from physical education because I was an athlete. As a result, I reached late adolescence with only a few informal gymnastics experiences. In college, as a physical education major in the late 1950s and early 1960s, I got to take two gymnastics courses, one in tumbling and one in apparatus. Both were presented very formally and progressively, using an Olympic system. I did learn good fundamental skills and good body mechanics, but I felt cheated! I never got to do gymnastics early enough or long enough to become competent in doing back handsprings, somersaults, and the like—the flashy stuff. And I never really felt satisfied because I never got to put a whole routine together. We learned and were tested on single skills.

When I started teaching I was convinced that gymnastics was good for children, and I began to search for ways to enhance my background. I attended workshops led by Joan Tillotson, Bette Jean Logsdon, Kate Barrett, John Wright, Jane Young, and Pat Tanner. I read all the British books on movement education I could get my hands on. I experienced a lot of personal growth in my knowledge of and teaching in all the physical education content areas—games, dance, movement concepts and motor skills, fitness, and gymnastics. The work of Rudolf Laban and the concepts of body, space, effort, and relationships became my main source of influence. Graduate work and a doctorate followed.

As I began teaching college in the early 1970s, college curriculums started to change. With the expansion of knowledge in disciplines such as exercise physiology and motor learning, content courses in skills were cut. As we enter the 1990s it is not unusual for physical education majors to receive but one course each in games, dance, and gymnastics. Often such courses earn just 1 credit and meet twice a week for the semester. How much gymnastics expertise can a teacher develop in one course? For years I have wrestled with the balance between the ideal and the reality. How can I give my students what they need to feel confident about teaching gymnastics to children?

For me, some answers emerged during a sabbatical in England in 1987. There I studied with Bob Smith of the Loughborough University of Technology. I also attended a national gymnastics conference where I heard John Wright of Nonington College, Martin Underwood of Exeter, Joyce Allen of the Chelsea School of Human Movement and others. Although gymnastics suffers the same plight—poor teaching and concern for safety—in England as in the United States, these leaders have taken a positive stance, bringing gymnastics into the 1990s to its rightful place in the national curriculum.

In a sense I have been accumulating the content of this book for over 30 years. These ideas represent my growth as a teacher. They combine my knowledge of gymnastics and of teaching.

They show where I am now. These ideas combine the best of developmental skills, health-related fitness, and conceptual learning derived from the field of human movement. They represent what I think is possible to do in the real world with gymnastics education.

In this book I want to present gymnastics in a way that has meaning for teachers. It is through you that children can enjoy the many developmental benefits of a gymnastics system focused on body management. This book is for both novice and experienced physical education teachers who want to enhance their background in gymnastics. The contents are packaged in two parts. Part I includes an introductory chapter that defines gymnastics, gives a brief history, and discusses how gymnastics contributes to the cognitive, affective, and psychomotor domains. Chapter 2 discusses adapting gymnastics to your teaching situation; and chapter 3, the three main skill themes of gymnastics. Next is a chapter giving principles for teaching the content and a chapter on both the process and the product of assessment.

The unique aspect of this book is the series of eight detailed learning experiences in Part II for each of the skill themes of traveling, statics, and rotation. Each learning experience follows a specific format that states the objectives, suggests an appropriate grade level, provides an organizational format, lists the necessary equipment, and describes the activity. The learning experiences conclude with points to watch for in student performances, ways to vary the lesson, and teachable moments, those times at the beginning, middle, or end of a learning experience that highlight selected points in the lesson. An appendix with sample routines, charts, awards, and letters to parents; a reference list; and an annotated list of suggested readings round out the book.

Most books on gymnastics present an Olympic menu of stunts, tumbling, and apparatus skills. A few texts follow an educational gymnastics format, using Laban's themes of body management. I have tried to give strength to this book by integrating Olympic and educational gymnastics in a way that challenges individuals and links gymnastics skills into meaningful sequences in each learning experience.

Any undertaking of this size cannot be done by one person. I am grateful, first, to all of the teachers and coaches, whose names you have read, for their contributions to my developing knowledge of gymnastics. In addition, I would like to thank Terry Sweeting, Sharon Brown, and Liz Jones, present or former graduate students, who have reviewed, taught, and made suggestions about lesson plans in the developmental phase of this book. Mary Werner prepared the tables and figures, and without her super job this book would have been void of aesthetic essentials. My thanks to Jodie Morris for correcting grammar and spelling as she typed the manuscript. My involvement with Scott Wikgren, Christine Hopple, and others at Human Kinetics has been superb. What a group of encouraging professionals! Finally, thanks to my family, Mary, Amy, and Lauren, who remained supportive and understanding through the long hours of writing and preparation.

Developmentally Appropriate Gymnastics

In 1992 the National Association for Sport and Physical Education (NASPE) published a document entitled *Developmentally Appropriate Physical Education Practices for Children*. The document, developed by the executive committee of the Council on Physical Education for Children (COPEC), represents the collective wisdom of many physical educators about what good elementary physical education is. The principles NASPE espoused in this document guided the development of this and the other four books in this series.

Part I begins with an overview of developmentally appropriate gymnastics, why it should be part of a quality elementary PE program, and how this approach differs from what has been traditionally taught in physical education. Chapter 1 also includes a definition of the physically educated person, including psychomotor, cognitive, and affective objectives, and a discussion of the significance of this definition for children's gymnastics instruction.

Virtually no two teaching situations are identical in physical education. Chapter 2 provides several suggestions on how you can structure your program to fit the idiosyncrasies of your school. This chapter includes ideas for teaching lessons with limited space, equipment, and time. As explained in this chapter, quality programs can be developed in less-than-ideal situations, but it's not easy.

A complete description of the content, including definitions of terms specific to the content area, is provided in chapter 3. As you review the content of all five books, you will quickly see that they contain much more than fun games and activities that are designed simply to keep children occupied for 30 minutes or so. Each content area outlines a developmentally appropriate curriculum designed to provide children with a logical progression of tasks leading to skillfulness in, and enjoyment of, physical activity.

Chapter 4 describes and discusses the key teaching principles that are used to provide developmentally appropriate experiences for children. This chapter applies pedagogical principles as they relate specifically to teaching the content included in the book. As you know, each of the five content areas has unique characteristics that master teachers are aware of as they teach their lessons.

The final chapter in Part I is on assessment. It describes practical ways to assess how well children are learning the concepts and skills related to the content being taught. As we enter the 21st century educators are increasingly being required to document, in realistic ways, the progress their children are making. This requirement presents unique challenges to the elementary school physical educator who may teach 600 or more children each week. Chapter 5 provides some realistic suggestions for ways to formatively assess what children are learning.

Chapter 1

Why Is It Important to Teach Children Gymnastics?

From infancy we are eager to master the possibilities of human movement. We crawl, we gain upright locomotion. We seek out ways to develop and vary our movement repertoire, venturing on to learn traveling, balancing, and rotation. Each of these skills is related to gymnastics in a broad sense.

When we were youngsters, my brother, my sister, and I would push back the sofa, chairs, and coffee table in the living room. My father would lie on his back and, one by one, lift us into the air. Sometimes we would stand on his hands and he would lift us into the air, other times he would support us horizontally with his feet at our waist. Often we would finish our acrobatics with rolls. Furniture occasionally would serve as a prop. We would lie on our backs on the seat, with our legs up over the back. We would reach our hands over our heads to the floor. From that position we would kick over, taking weight on our hands, and land in a squat position on our feet. It was great fun, and we would gleefully cry, One more time! Watch me!

I remember many similar activities outdoors: My dad holding me firmly by the arms to spin me round and round. Riding high up on someone's shoulders. Rolling down a grassy hill. Doing cartwheels on the lawn. Climbing trees. Jumping over logs in the woods. Playing on the jungle gym. Swinging from grapevines. Crossing a creek or brook, jumping from one rock to another. Sliding down an icy hill in winter by spinning on a plastic saucer. Walking on the railroad tracks, trying to keep balanced. Hanging upside down from a tree limb or playground ladder. We loved to ride the swing, slide, merry-go-round, and see-saw.

Although children's play equipment has changed over the years, the intent has not. As a child I used to jump a Lemon Twist, walk on stilts, jump on pogo sticks, walk on Romper Stompers, and use a hula hoop. Today's children use skateboards, snowboards, roller blades, scooter boards, pogo balls, and hoppity hops. All these activities that emphasize traveling and balancing are great fun.

Children of all ages seem fascinated by rides which stimulate their vestibular awareness (sense of balance) and their body's position in space. Youngsters enjoy elevators and escalators. Carnival rides and theme-park rides, such as the Tilt-A-Whirl, Scrambler, Magic Mountain, roller coaster, and Ferris wheel stimulate our awareness of linear and rotary motion. We can't seem to get enough.

In years of the Olympic games there is a huge increase in the number of parents who enroll their children in gymnastics centers. Girls dream of becoming Mary Lou Retton, Kathy Rigby, Nadia Comaneci, Olga Korbut, Shannon Miller,

Kim Zmeskal, or Betty Okino. Boys dream of becoming Bart Conner, Kurt Thomas, Mitsou Toukahara, Vitaly Sherbo, Mitch Gaylord, or Trent Dimas (see Figure 1.1). Other children pursue gymnastics to become cheerleaders, acrobats, or circus clowns.

Despite the excitement and challenge of moving our bodies in different ways, only a handful of children pursue gymnastics beyond childhood. These are the elite few who aspire to the Olympics, although many youngsters use gymnastics skills as an avenue toward cheerleading.

Gymnastics plays a role in sports and everyday life by helping people learn to manage their bodies efficiently and safely. A bicycle rider, seeing a dog suddenly cross his path, tumbles to the ground, rolls, and staves off serious injury. A painter miscalculates a rung on a short ladder, stumbles, but recovers before total disaster. A softball player runs, makes a diving catch, rolls, and comes up throwing to catch the runner at first. A football player gets blocked, rolls back to his feet, pursues, and makes the tackle. All use variations of gymnastics movements, by people who are not Olympic gymnasts.

Defining Developmentally Appropriate Gymnastics

Gymnastics may be globally defined as any physical exercise on the floor or apparatus that is designed to promote endurance, strength, flexibility, agility, coordination, and body control. At its best, it is body management using functional movement to master the body. As such it is different from games, which promote the mastering of objects and the accomplishment of a purpose such as overcoming an opponent, and from dance, which promotes the expression or communication of feelings, attitudes, ideas, and concepts.

Gymnastics is like many other childhood activities, however, in that it includes learning to develop locomotor and balance skills, as well as body and space awareness. Beyond enhancing an individual's body awareness, gymnastics is an activity involving movement in a controlled manner. It is also an enjoyable aesthetic activity that uses a variety of stimuli (apparatus, group work, music) to promote development of the body and mind to answer specific tasks.

A physical education program featuring gymnastics benefits children in many areas. It improves body management and control and aids the development of locomotive, nonlocomotive, and manipulative skills. It promotes endurance, strength, flexibility, agility, and coordination. These abilities in turn relate to health and fitness. In addition, gymnastics can improve cognitive and affective outcomes in the areas of problem solving, body mechanics, and aesthetics. I will develop each of these components as outcomes later in more depth; but first, some observations on the history of gymnastics may demonstrate how it can benefit a physical education curriculum.

Figure 1.1 Many children dream of performing in the Olympics.

Brief History of Gymnastics

As early as 2600 BC the Chinese practiced a series of medical exercises called Kung Fu. They thought diseases resulted from inactivity of the body and developed medical gymnastics, or Kung Fu, to combine movements with breathing exercises to help the organs function, prolong life, and ensure the soul's immortality.

The Greek culture also developed the body/mind concept. Philosophers such as Socrates, Plato, and Aristotle promoted physical training, seeking beauty, strength, and efficiency in movement. Hints of medical gymnastics, massage, and health-related fitness trace back to classical Greece.

In the Roman empire, society promoted physical activity to facilitate military training of its male citizens. As a result, Roman youths developed strength, stamina, and courage through physical conditioning. Among the array of sports activities—which included ball games, running, jumping, and throwing—acrobatics appeared as a form of gymnastics.

In the early nineteenth century European schools began to develop for all classes of society. Physical education played an integral role in the curriculum. In Germany, Johann Friedrich Guts-Muth, and later Friedrich Ludwig Jahn, used physical education to further political aspirations toward nationhood and freedom from the repression of Napoleonic France. Jahn's system of gymnastics was widely adopted at outdoor and indoor gymnastics centers, marking the beginning of modern Olympic gymnastics. Schoolboys performed gymnastics exercises regularly in the hope that sovereignty would follow the development of strong, sturdy, and fearless German youths. They saw a direct link between gymnastics and fitness, or a military gymnastics.

Nationalism also motivated Sweden's P.H. Ling to develop a physical education system. Ling hoped that a vigorous youth would help recapture Sweden's dignity following its loss of territory in wars with Russia in the late 1700s and early 1800s. He also thought that his gymnastics system, based on an extensive study of anatomy and physiology, would enhance aesthetic, educational, and health values. The Swedish gymnastics system was based on apparatus work, including swinging ladders and rings, rope climbing, and vaulting bars and stall bars. Careful attention was given to the development of exercises in progression from simple to complex.

Before the mid-nineteenth century there was no formal physical education in the United States. Puritanical religious beliefs and harsh living conditions allowed little time for recreation and pleasure. A notable exception was the development of the Jahn Turnverein gymnastics program in Massachusetts in the mid 1830s. At that time Catherine Bucher adapted German gymnastics in the U.S., developing a system of simpler, lighter calisthenic exercises done to music. Bucher's work resulted in the birth of rhythmic gymnastics.

Between the 1870s and World War I military training had an obvious influence on the physical preparedness of young men. At the same time there was more concern for preventive medicine. As a result, leaders such as Dio Lewis, Edward Hitchcock, and Dudley Sargent promoted both German and Swedish gymnastics programs in the United States.

Another important figure in the development of informal or educational gymnastics came from Germany just prior to World War II. Rudolf Laban fled from Germany to England, establishing himself as a leader in modern dance there. He developed movement themes based on body and space awareness, effort, and relationships (BSER). His thematic approach to movement encouraged individuals to solve and interpret movement problems in new and creative ways. Laban's influence carried over into gymnastics and games; movement education programs became popular in England.

At this time Liselott Diem in Germany developed programs based on exploration of structured environments using gymnastics apparatus. Her programs subsequently gained widespread popularity in the United States and other parts of the world in the 1960s.

Movement education is a significant departure from previous programs in physical education. Unlike the more structured system of progressive content development, in which all students are expected to perform to the same standard, educational gymnastics encourages individuals to resolve movement problems in unique ways that correspond to their ability levels. For example, rather than have all students attempt a headstand, teachers may ask children to find a way to balance in an inverted position on three body parts.

Gymnastics has branched in many different directions over the years. It is the umbrella (see Figure 1.2) that includes many forms of movement, much as dance assumes different forms

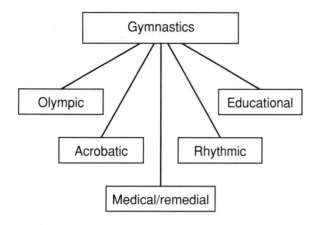

Figure 1.2   The many branches of gymnastics.

(jazz, tap, modern, folk, square, ballet, aerobic). Clearly, it is for the teacher to decide which elements of gymnastics are most appropriate in given situations.

Where Are We Now?

Gymnastics, as traditionally defined, is almost dead in public schools across America. Children learn the same forward roll, backward roll, and cartwheel in every grade level from K to 12. As they repeat these skills each year, some children get increasingly bored. Others never master the simpler skills to standard and feel they are no good. Some students fall and get injured attempting skills they have no business trying. These children become fearful and refuse to continue.

It is no wonder we find educators asking whether gymnastics should have a prominent place in the school curriculum and what its benefits are. How can we present gymnastics to maintain children's enthusiasm and motivate high levels of participation?

Some of the reasons people question the validity of gymnastics—despite its rich history in medicine, hygiene, fitness, Olympic sports, body management, problem solving, and acrobatics—trace back to college curricula. Over the last 30 years physical education programs have added such courses as sports psychology, motor learning, exercise physiology, and biomechanics. The total number of hours in the major, however, has not increased proportionally. As a result students have time to take only one content course in gymnastics, perhaps neglecting stunts and tumbling, apparatus, and rhythmic or educational training. It is difficult then for teachers

to present a content area confidently and well, having very little background in that area. Teachers are confused. Should they teach Olympic? educational? by direct methods? indirect or problem solving methods?

In fact, there are excellent aspects of each approach to gymnastics. The strength of Olympic gymnastics is the progressive development of skill. Educational gymnastics allows for individual differences, focusing on problem-solving and developing body management skills. We can teach Olympic gymnastics with both direct and indirect teaching styles. The same is true of educational gymnastics. Because of time constraints gymnastics at the elementary school level should focus on entry-level skills rather than more tangential pursuits such as acrobatics and modern rhythmic gymnastics. Sound basic skills are more important than an exposure to several gymnastics systems, without enough time to do any of them justice.

How Gymnastics Should Be Taught

To teach a system of basic body management and gymnastics skills well, we should be aware of some recent research on teaching and the study of content knowledge, particularly on how gymnastics should be taught (Graham, 1992; Shulman, 1987). If we want children to become skilled gymnasts with positive attitudes toward managing their bodies well, we must adhere to the following practices.

Begin With Knowledge of Skill Components

Content knowledge is very important. Although you needn't be an expert performer to teach a skill, there is no substitute for knowing how it is performed. Otherwise you have no idea what to look for, what performance cues to give, how to evaluate a child's performance, or what to correct. Imagine a teacher trying to teach the cartwheel. She says, "You put your hands down, then your feet." An inaccurate demonstration by the teacher or a selected child follows. Children begin practicing. Some succeed. Others crash to the floor with arms and legs bent and out of control. "Try again, you can do better," the teacher encourages. But poor form continues.

The children obviously need a better model. Because the cartwheel is sequential, performance cues like these are needed: "Start in a wide stretch, with your arms and legs stretched like spokes in a wheel. Place hand, then hand, then foot, then foot on the ground. Start and finish facing the same direction. Keep your arms and legs straight. Try to get your shoulders over your hands and your hips over your shoulders when you are upside down. Push hard with your hands and arms as you return to your feet. Keep your body tight. Land softly on your feet."

Allow Considerable Practice Time

Children need lengthy and appropriate practice to learn skills like a roll, a cartwheel, a balance, or a sequence involving a balance, weight transfer, and a second balance. When we line students up and spot them one by one, they may only get one or two practices before moving on to a new skill—the rest of the time they are waiting in line. This is not a good use of teaching time.

Let's examine a common format for teaching the forward roll, the backward roll, and the log roll. Children are lined up in squads at each of four mats. They listen to an explanation, watch a demonstration, and begin to practice. Each takes a turn and returns to the end of the line. After three tries, they learn the next roll. Their total practice is only nine attempts—three times on three rolls.

Although each roll may be taught with an excellent explanation and demonstration, the children aren't getting enough practice to capitalize on the good instruction. These children could get much more practice in if you were to reorganize the class, perhaps by assigning partners to go back and forth across the mat or by having one mat for every two students or carpet squares for every child in open or scatter formation.

Use Developmentally Appropriate Activities

Student satisfaction results from success. High success rates on tasks and a student's general achievement are positively correlated. When a task is too hard or above their ability level children become frustrated, giving up or engaging in off-task behavior. You can design tasks or movement problems to allow for differences in the children's individual levels. When tasks are at appropriate levels, students will be challenged. Rather than require an entire class to do a headstand for 10 seconds or a handspring, it would be more appropriate to work on balances in inverted positions or the transfer of weight from the feet to the hands and back to the feet. For example, some students may do reasonably well learning backward rolls, while others have a great deal of difficulty because their arms are weak, their head gets in the way, or they open up instead of staying tucked.

Consider modifying the task for students who have difficulty. For example, using a backward roll over the shoulder eases the move. Another alternative is to work on the concept of rolling in general, showing students how to transfer body weight from one adjacent body part to another. After they learn this concept, then children could roll choosing a direction and style that they can accomplish successfully. Once a roll is mastered, challenge the children to link a roll with a balance or a traveling action, taking the skill to a higher level of difficulty.

Encourage Cognitive and Affective Development

Rich learning environments are important to engage children both cognitively and affectively. Children need to learn good body mechanics and understand why one balance is better than another. To challenge their minds children need tasks that require resolution. They need to examine which movements link together well. Children need to work together with peers, giving and receiving feedback on form, suggesting alternatives to movements, and helping each other perform new skills (see Figure 1.3).

Often teachers ask children to do predesigned skills or sequences without allowing them input and choice in the matter. Instead of specifying a scale into a forward roll or a roundoff into a backward roll, try designing open-ended movement tasks. For example, you could say to the children, "Perform a balance of your choice and hold it for 3 seconds. Move smoothly into a rolling action. Finish with a second balance. Or take weight momentarily on your hands and, as you return to your feet, perform a roll of your choice." As children make choices of which skills link together more smoothly and which skills look and feel more aesthetically pleasing, and as they give and receive feedback from partners, they gain an appreciation for, and begin to value, what it takes to be a quality gymnast. This is the essence of affective development. They could work alone or with a partner to develop good responses to this direction.

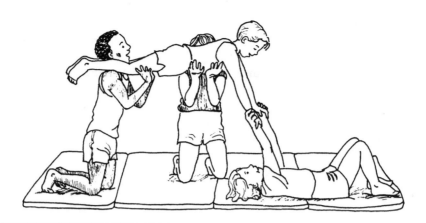

Figure 1.3 Children can assist, cooperate, and give suggestions on improving form.

Offer a Structured Environment

A structured or focused learning environment helps children understand goals. When teachers set goals, children know what is expected. The children know what to do and how to do it. Goals also make children accountable when the time comes for assessment.

Some teachers assign several balance positions in no apparent order and for no apparent reason. Children learn a scale, stork stand, tip-up, and a tripod. They practice a hodgepodge of animal walks, such as the crab walk, bear walk, and mule kicks. By putting these balances and movements into logical sets, a teacher helps her students understand why they learn them.

At the beginning of the gymnastics unit or lesson, give students a brief orientation. Tell them what to expect. "Gymnastics is about putting balances together with traveling actions, weight transfers, and rotations." You might add a demonstration. This way the students receive a clear picture of the goal for the day or the unit.

These are exciting times to be teaching, particularly to be involved in teaching gymnastics. With the interest in restructuring education, it has been a time to question where we have been, what we know, and where we would like to go.

At the international level, there is a movement to link gymnastics with healthy living and active lifestyles (The Physical Education Association of Great Britain and Northern Ireland, 1991). British educators are debating the concept of gymnastics as health-related fitness for life. In many European countries gymnastics has become a leisure and fitness activity. German gymnastics clubs consist of large recreational sports complexes, centers for self-improvement with a strong emphasis on the physical well-being of members. In other European countries rhythmical gymnastics (work to music) is the most common type of fitness class. National festivals display various techniques such as *Lingiades, Turnfests, Spartakiades,* and *Gymnaestrades.*

Let's bring this festival spirit to the local level. Imagine in your school gymnasium a fitness night for parents and children, a field day with gymnastics in the spotlight. This occasion would focus on a holistic approach to gymnastics, incorporating movement criteria; natural activities; dynamic, static, and flow concepts; and a stimulating environment with apparatus and music. It might be the impetus to help gymnastics regain prominence in the school curriculum.

Outcome Goals for Gymnastics

Physical education leaders in recent years (Franck et al., 1991; The Physical Education Association of Great Britain and Northern Ireland, 1991) have called for quality, daily classes in which children can develop optimally in the psychomotor, cognitive, and affective domains. The National Association for Sport and Physical Education in their Outcomes Project (Franck et al., 1991) has defined a physically educated person and the outcomes of a quality physical education program (see Figure 1.4).

NASPE identifies sample, grade-specific competencies they call *benchmarks* in gymnastics (see Figure 1.5). Using these benchmarks as goals can help teachers assess their students' progress in becoming physically educated. The learning experiences you will read in Part II are based, in part, on these benchmarks.

Let's examine how participating in gymnastics contributes specifically to an individual's

A Physically Educated Person:

- **Has** learned skills necessary to perform a variety of physical activities:
    1. Moves using concepts of body awareness, space awareness, effort and relationships
    2. Demonstrates competence in a variety of manipulative, locomotor and non-locomotor skills
    3. Demonstrates competence in combinations of manipulative, locomotor and non-locomotor skills performed individually and with others
    4. Demonstrates competence in many different forms of physical activity
    5. Demonstrates proficiency in a few forms of physical activity
    6. Has learned how to learn new skills

- **Is** physically fit:
    7. Assesses, achieves and maintains physical fitness
    8. Designs safe, personal fitness programs in accordance with principles of training and conditioning

- **Does** participate regularly in physical activity:
    9. Participates in health-enhancing physical activity at least three times a week
    10. Selects and regularly participates in lifetime physical activities

- **Knows** the implications of and the benefits from involvement in physical activities:
    11. Identifies the benefits, costs and obligations associated with regular participation in physical activity
    12. Recognizes the risk and safety factors associated with regular participation in physical activity
    13. Applies concepts and principles to the development of motor skills
    14. Understands that wellness involves more than being physically fit
    15. Knows the rules, strategies and appropriate behaviors for selected physical activities
    16. Recognizes that participation in physical activity can lead to multi-cultural and international understanding
    17. Understands that physical activity provides the opportunity for enjoyment, self-expression and communication

- **Values** physical activity and its contributions to a healthful lifestyle:
    18. Appreciates the relationships with others that result from participation in physical activity
    19. Respects the role that regular physical activity plays in the pursuit of life-long health and well-being
    20. Cherishes the feelings that result from regular participation in physical activity

Figure 1.4 Outcomes of quality physical education programs. *Note.* The "Physically Educated Person" document containing these outcomes and accompanying benchmarks (see Figure 1.4) can be obtained by contacting NASPE at 1900 Association Drive, Reston, VA 22091-1599 or by calling 1-800-321-0789.
From *Physical Education Outcomes: A Project of the National Association for Sport and Physical Education* by M. Franck, G. Graham, H. Lawson, T. Loughrey, R. Ritson, M. Sanborn, and V. Seefeldt (The Outcomes Committee of NASPE), 1991. Reprinted by permission of the National Association for Sport and Physical Education, Reston, VA.

development in light of these outcome and benchmark statements.

Psychomotor Domain

In the psychomotor domain outcomes and benchmarks address skill and physiological development: Review the *has*, *is*, and *does* statements in the NASPE outcomes project in Figures 1.4 and 1.5.

Skill Development

The wide range of movement activities that children experience in gymnastics can be categorized

As a result of participating in a quality education program, it is reasonable to expect that the student will be able to do the following:

Psychomotor Domain (Has, Is, Does)

Roll sideways (right or left) without hesitating or stopping (K, #9)

Place a variety of body parts into low, medium, and high levels (K, #7)

Move feet into high level by placing the weight on the hands (1-2, #8)

Jump and land using a combination of one and two foot takeoffs and landings (1-2, #4)

Roll smoothly in a forward direction without stopping or hesitating (1-2, #6)

Combine shapes, levels, and pathways into simple sequences (1-2, #17)

Roll, in a backward direction, without hesitating or stopping (3-4, #3)

Transfer weight from feet to hands, at fast and slow speeds using large extensions (e.g., mule kick, handstand, cartwheel) (3-4, #4)

Design gymnastics sequences that are personally interesting (3-4, #26)

Design and perform gymnastics and dance sequences that combine traveling, rolling, balancing, and weight transfer into smooth, flowing sequences with intentional changes in direction, speed, and flow (5-6, #4)

Move each joint through a full range of motion (1-2, #19)

Manage own body weight while hanging and climbing (1-2, #20)

Support, lift, and control body weight in a variety of activities (3-4, #16)

Correctly demonstrate activities designed to improve and maintain muscular strength and endurance, flexibility, and cardiorespiratory functioning (5-6, #15)

Cognitive Domain (Knows)

State guidelines and behaviors for the safe use of equipment and apparatus (K, #21)

Identify ways movement concepts can be used to refine movement skills (3-4, #21)

Describe essential elements of mature movement patterns (3-4, #23)

Analyze potential risks associated with physical activities (3-4, #25)

Detect, analyze, and correct errors in personal movement patterns (5-6, #24)

Affective Domain (Values)

Accept the feelings that result from challenges, successes, and failures in physical activity (1-2, #28)

Seek out, participate with, and show respect for persons of like and different skill levels (5-6, #27)

Figure 1.5   Sample benchmarks relevant for gymnastics. The first number in parentheses following each benchmark relates to the grade level(s) it can be found under in the NASPE document, the second number gives the specific benchmark for that grade level. These will be used in reference to objectives for each learning experience in Part II, as appropriate. See page 47 for further information.

Note. From *Physical Education Outcomes: A Project of the National Association for Sport and Physical Education* by M. Franck, G. Graham, H. Lawson, T. Loughrey, R. Ritson, M. Sanborn, and V. Seefeldt (The Outcomes Committee of NASPE), 1991. Adapted by permission of the National Association for Sport and Physical Education, Reston, VA.

as locomotion—or traveling, statics, and rotation (I will develop these concepts in more detail in Chapter 3). The important point here is that early experiences should develop basic skills; in time, the tasks become more complex and more difficult. Some basic skills, for example, are traveling on the feet, balancing, and rolling. Learning concepts of body awareness and space awareness helps children develop a variety of movement responses to use with given challenges or tasks. Children can also work on refining these basic movement responses.

As children become more competent, additional concepts focusing on effort actions and relationships are gradually added. In general, levels of skill proficiency should form the guidelines (Graham, 1992). In the early elementary grades children, operating at a pre-control and control level, work on skills to become efficient, effective, and adaptable movers under simple conditions. In practical terms, they will run, jump, land, roll, and balance, focusing on these skills individually. They may begin to put the skills together into simple sequences. In the upper elementary grades, as children approach utilization and proficiency levels, their increasing competence allows students to work on more difficult skills. They can put skills together in sequences and work in more complex relationships with partners, small groups, and equipment or apparatus.

Physiological Development

Physiological development in gymnastics is concerned with health-related fitness concepts. Over time, work units in gymnastics should emphasize cardiorespiratory development, muscular strength and endurance, and flexibility. During periods of warm-up, children can derive cardiorespiratory benefits by running, hopping, skipping, and jumping. They can also use traveling actions to approach—jump onto, along, and off—benches, boxes, beams, and other pieces of equipment to attain continuous movement. Continuous repetition of simple sequences, such as running on the floor and rolling or wheeling across mats, can also achieve a cardiorespiratory effect. The critical factor is to keep people moving in a gymnastic, aesthetic manner. This is not jogging, a race, or aerobic dance. It is being a gymnast who is moving continuously: running, jumping, vaulting, and rolling with good mechanics.

Cardiorespiratory fitness does not take place in a vacuum, however. It cannot be achieved in a 1- or 2-day-a-week program or in a 5-minute warm-up. When gymnastics is combined with other efforts such as fitness breaks during the school day, walking and running programs, and an active over-all program, it will contribute toward cardiorespiratory development.

Focusing on the strength of different muscle groups can be a part of the conditioning phase of each lesson. Taking weight on the hands builds muscles in the arms and shoulder girdle. Making bridges with the body, supporting the body's weight in front and rear support positions, and holding balance positions also develop arm strength. Rolling, rocking, balancing, traveling on the feet, and vaulting develop muscles of the abdomen, buttocks, and legs. Most gymnastics skills require strong, tight bodies for control. Lifting, supporting, and propelling the body into the air each requires a tremendous amount of strength. Done repetitively over time, these activities develop endurance as well.

During the conditioning and cool-down phases of a lesson, body flexibility can be developed and maintained. It is important for gymnasts to have a good range of motion in all of the joints. Straddle and pike positions, back bends, happy and angry cat positions and various other actions promote flexibility of the shoulder, back, hip, and ankle joints.

Cognitive Domain

In the cognitive domain outcomes and benchmarks address basic knowledge and higher-order thinking skills. For development in the cognitive domain review the *knows* statements in the NASPE outcomes project in Figures 1.4 and 1.5.

Basic Knowledge

Gymnastics should provide children a variety of experiences to develop cognitive abilities. At the simplest level children can acquire a knowledge of their body parts and how to move them in and through space. Their movements should reflect a knowledge of shape, level, direction, pathway, extension, time, force, flow, and relationships (body and space awareness, effort, and relationships [BSER] framework). Over time, children should learn a variety of biomechanical principles such as rotation, center of gravity, base of support, levers, balance, counterbalance, momentum, and force application.

Higher-Order Thinking Skills

As children develop basic movement skills, present them with opportunities for higher-order thinking skills. Open-ended, process-oriented tasks provide opportunities to solve problems by developing the students' comprehension and abilities to apply, analyze, synthesize, and evaluate movement. For example, have the children think of a balance with a wide base and low center of gravity. Next, let them do a balance with a wide base and a high center of gravity. Then ask them, "Which one is more stable? why?" You can also ask the children to create a movement sequence using each of the body's three axes for rotation. Ask the children what the three axes are and which skills they used for rotation around each axis. The program in gymnastics should be an education in both motor skills and movement understanding.

Affective Domain

In the affective domain outcomes and benchmarks address aesthetic and creative development: Review the *values* statements in the NASPE outcomes project in Figures 1.4 and 1.5.

Aesthetic Development

Gymnastics does not have the same aesthetic concerns as dance. Dancers are concerned with the body as an instrument of expression. Gymnasts are more concerned with the function of movement. The beauty of gymnastics movement derives from a concern for the shape and line of action. Gymnasts strive to link actions, or to create a flow of action from one movement to another. There is a kinesthetic satisfaction in performing an action just right. In terms of outcomes gymnasts know and apply movement concepts and principles to achieve a satisfying, proficient, aesthetic performance of a single skill or a sequence. As observers and appraisers gymnasts also can appreciate watching the movement of others.

Creative Development

True creativity in gymnastics is relatively rare, for there are only so many ways the body can move. New moves (such as the Endo or Toukahara) sometimes are invented and christened. With children, however, creativity means putting together a series of movements, which may be novel to the individual. Rather than always telling youngsters what skills to perform and in what order, it is wise sometimes to give children choices. Perform a roll and finish in a balance. Choose a traveling action to approach and mount the bench, balance on the bench using a symmetrical (or asymmetrical) shape, and exit the bench with a rolling (sliding or wheeling) action.

Psychological Development

Children learn what they can and cannot do with their bodies. In a gymnastics system that promotes body management children will discover appropriate challenges within their ability level. Challenges require some risk-taking, courage, and perseverance. If you present tasks, lessons, and units in a logical sequence, children will challenge themselves to do their best work, overcome some fears, learn their limits, and probably develop a healthy measure of self-esteem.

Summary

Gymnastics is at a crossroads in public school education. It has a rich history of contributing to healthy lifestyles, yet because of several factors has not figured significantly in the physical education curriculum for several decades. Recently educators have called for reforms to redefine quality in daily physical education. Gymnastics has much to contribute to children's development in skills, physiological, aesthetic, creative, psychological, and cognitive areas. It should once again be an integral part of elementary school physical education.

Chapter 2

Tailoring Gymnastics to Fit Your Teaching Situation

Teaching would be much easier if all schools and all grade levels were identical. Then a standardized curriculum with detailed lesson plans would work everywhere. The fact is, however, that our teaching situations have some similarities—and some definite differences! These differences include class size, facilities, class frequency, equipment, length of the class period, the community, and a broad range of ages, abilities, and special needs within the same class of children. This chapter briefly describes some ways the content in this book can be adapted to various teaching situations to best meet the needs of the children and also to heighten their enjoyment and learning.

Class Size

Although it is recommended that "physical education classes contain the same number of children as the classrooms (e.g., 25 children per class)" (Council on Physical Education for Children, 1992), some schools and districts schedule two or three classes at the same time, which means the PE teacher must teach 60 or more children simultaneously. Although this makes the teacher's job difficult, there are ways teachers can develop the content to provide children with positive (albeit far from ideal) learning experiences. For example, the use of stations, or learning centers, is probably one of the more efficient ways to organize large groups of children (Graham, 1992). And using written directions can minimize the time spent talking to the children, who often seem less inclined to listen when they are in large groups. Also, the teacher must devote substantial time to teaching management routines (Siedentop, 1991) or protocols (Graham, 1992) so that classes are run efficiently with minimal interruptions.

In order for students both to receive individual attention and to work in safe environments, class sizes should be kept as small as possible. About 25 students (which is normal for most classrooms) is a good number to work with (see Figure 2.1). With larger class sizes or where children are divided into smaller groups for station works, parents and upper-level elementary children can be trained to help supervise, assist, or spot for selected skills.

Equipment

One reason why large class sizes are *not* recommended is that most physical education programs do not have sufficient equipment—not even for 25 or 30 children. Consequently, if teachers are not careful, the children spend

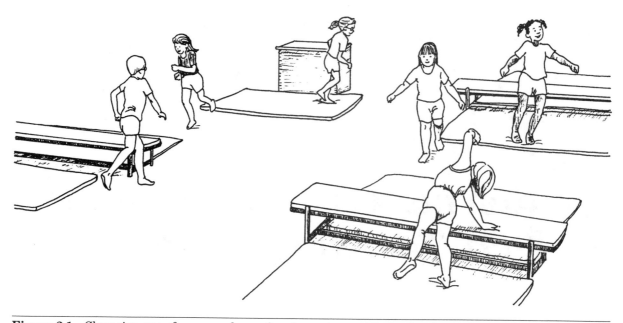

Figure 2.1   Class size, use of space, and use of equipment are critical safety issues in gymnastics.

considerable time waiting for turns rather than actually moving. But innovative teachers have discovered ways to maximize practice opportunities for children, even with limited equipment.

Regarding gymnastics equipment, the more you have (within reason) the better off you are. Don't get disheartened, however: You can build an excellent gymnastics program for body management and health-related fitness using mats and benches, or boxes.

If you have only three to five 4' × 6' mats with which to work, you need to develop a plan. You might buy one or two more each year, meanwhile substituting carpet squares or old bed mattresses. The school's PTA may be willing to do a special fund raiser or event for the purchase of mats or a piece of apparatus. You could also share equipment with the local park recreation department or other schools within the district. Try setting up a rotation schedule in the fall with each school contributing two or more mats; collectively there should be enough for one school's program at a time.

If you have no benches or boxes now, develop a plan to purchase one or two a year until you have sufficient equipment. Perhaps you can contract with the high school shop class to design and build the benches and boxes. (See the plans for constructing boxes and benches in Graham, Holt/Hale, & Parker, 1993). In the meantime you can substitute tables and chairs, commercial milk crates, wooden boxes, and cardboard boxes filled with newspapers. Define your purpose.

Perhaps you need equipment for balancing or jumping. Choose something that will allow you to accomplish the purpose successfully and safely (see Table 2.1).

After you have mats, benches, and boxes, you will want to expand the gymnastics program, eventually providing opportunities for children to hang, swing, support their body weight, balance, spring, vault, and so on. Purchasing balance beams, parallel bars, horizontal bars, and trampettes supports these gymnastics movement skills. Build toward this goal, but don't give up and say you can't teach gymnastics because you don't have an ideal situation. Do the best you can with what you have. As interest in the program grows, parents and school administrators will support it.

After acquiring gymnastics equipment, it is important to think about its organization and arrangement. It is tempting to put mats, benches, and boxes in nice straight rows and columns. Having everything neat and orderly helps us feel good as teachers. There are more important goals to consider in placing equipment, however. We should arrange a natural flow from one piece of equipment to another, setting the pieces to link actions between one activity or skill and another. One such arrangement is shown in Figure 2.2.

Facilities

Although some teachers have adequate indoor and outdoor space, others are less fortunate. In

Table 2.1 Alternative Equipment

Piece	Specifications	Suggested uses
Boxes—from school cafeteria, empty cases of school paper	12"-18" high 18"-24" long and wide Filled with newspaper Ends sealed with masking tape	Jump onto, off of, over Balance on completely or partially Roll onto, off of Cartwheel over
Benches	12"-18" high 10'-12' long 10"-12" wide Base wide, stable to prevent tipping	Travel along Balance on Jump onto, off of, over Roll along, onto, off of Cartweel over, off of
Tables	2'-3' high 24"-36" wide 6'-8' long Stable, sturdy non-folding	Balance on completely or partially Roll off of Jump off
Chairs	Stable, sturdy Four legs, back	Balance on Vault over Jump onto, off of
Plastic crates—milk, soft drink	6"-18" high 18"-24" long and wide Place upside down on mats or other nonskid surfaces	Balance on Jump over, onto, off of Roll onto, off of Cartwheel over

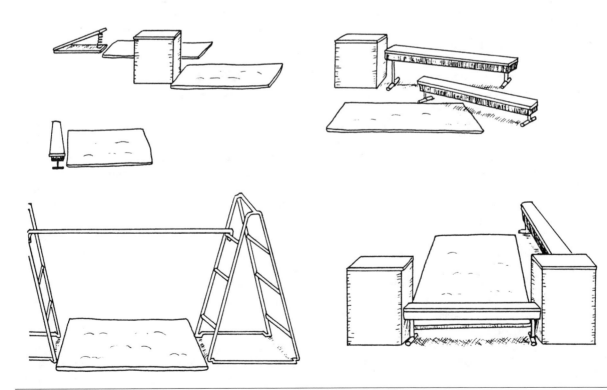

Figure 2.2 Arrange equipment to provide a natural flow from one piece to the next.

fact, some teachers have no indoor space whatsoever. Others have no grassy areas. Following are some ideas and suggestions for how the content in this book can be adapted for limited indoor or outdoor space.

Who wouldn't want to teach children in Bela Karolyi's gym and have all the best equipment money can buy? A large, open exercise space with the latest cushioned mat, multiple beams, bars, horses—whouldn't they be great! I recall a friend in graduate school who once declared, "A master fencer could teach fencing with broom handles better than I could with all of the latest models of foils." The point is that we need to make the best of our present situation but build toward the future.

An open space is critical to teaching gymnastics safely and successfully. Children need space to run, jump, land, roll, balance, and practice all the other gymnastic skills. There must be enough space between pieces of equipment to execute skills without bumping into the walls, other children, or equipment. A large gymnasium or multipurpose room is the dream of gymnastics teachers. Gymnastics can be taught, however, on school stages, in empty classrooms, or hallways, with some compromises. These kinds of spaces usually are much smaller, so safety and participation levels become concerns. You have to judge how many children can safely participate at a time in a given area. If children are spending inordinate time in lines and waiting turns, you may wish to make alternative plans. One solution is to split groups, assigning two or more activities. One group outside might do a ball skill, or jump rope, while the other group is inside doing gymnastics. When a class is split into two or more groups, volunteers, parents, or teacher aides can supervise one activity. Another solution is to move gymnastics outdoors.

Teaching gymnastics outside is not ideal, but it is workable. In the South, where many schools often do not have gyms, there may be no other choice. Practicing gymnastics on a blacktop surface, with or without the protection of a roof, on the playground, or on an open grassy area can be difficult. You need to be creative. Moving mats and equipment outside and back inside every day is a management nightmare. Children can help, especially students who arrive at school early and take the late bus home, if they are taught how to carry mats in and out safely (see protocols, Graham, 1992). Large parachutes can be placed on outside grass or dirt surfaces to help protect skin and clothes. Organization is the key.

Class Frequency and Length

Schools and classes differ in the number of days per week that the children attend physical education classes and the length of the classes. Children who have physical education every day for 30 minutes can be expected to learn more than children who only have 60 minutes of physical education each week. This is one reason it is virtually impossible to suggest a standardized physical education curriculum. As suggested in the section later in this chapter on planning, you will need to consider these factors as you plan. Aim to organize and teach your classes so that if students have physical education twice a week for 30 minutes, they receive more than 16 hours of actual learning time each year (Kelly, 1989).

Each of the gymnastics learning experiences includes suggested beginning or warm-up activities, new skills, and the integration of newly acquired skills with other skill themes to develop sequences, or routines. If children already have some background, such as doing simple rolls or individual balances well, they might accomplish a given learning experience in one class period. In other instances, such as taking weight on the hands or achieving partner balances, a learning experience may take several class periods or even comprise a short unit. It is important to develop quality movement and build skill. There is no sense in moving on before fundamental skills are mastered. This is a key to ensuring safety.

Accommodating Individual Differences

Many classes today have children with special needs who are mainstreamed (i.e., their physical education class is scheduled with another class). In some instances you can accommodate children with special needs (not only those who are mainstreamed), by techniques such as *teaching by invitation* or *intratask variation* (Graham, 1992; see Figure 2.3). In other instances it may be necessary to make different adaptations to accommodate the needs of these students. Some accommodations that teachers can make for children when teaching gymnastics are discussed in this section.

Children with special needs in gymnastics should be taught on a specific basis, using an Individualized Education Plan (IEP). In many instances, a hearing-impaired or blind child can work as a partner with another child who will

Figure 2.3 Intratask variations can accommodate individual differences in skill or ability. Compare (a) child with low skill doing a simple forward roll with (b) child with high skill doing a forward straddle roll.

assist the impaired child in performing a skill or sequence. Visual demonstrations can show hearing-impaired children what to do. A teacher can modify tasks in many ways to fit an individual's needs. For example, a child in a wheelchair can make shapes with the arms and upper torso and do rotations with a spin of the chair. Tasks can be made easier for the low-skilled, obese, or nonambulatory child as well. Instead of doing rolls, cartwheels, or springing and vaulting actions, less able children can practice a seated roll or simple arm weight-bearing tasks.

Community Needs

Another consideration is the characteristics of the community in which you teach. This includes not only the city or town but also the community of the school. Religious concerns may influence the content (e.g., some religions have prohibitions on dancing). In northern states ice skating or snow skiing may be part of the content to be taught. Some principals (who have yet to be fully educated about quality physical education) may have concerns about what content is (or is not) taught. Increasingly, for example, the safety of gymnastics is being questioned.

- Educate the principal, teachers, and parents you work with about gymnastics. Emphasize that it develops health-related fitness and body management. It is for all children, not just an elite few.

- Found the program on sound and safe practices. Build skills and confidence on the floor before moving to equipment. Develop the children's self-control with good body mechanics. Gymnastics should not place children at risk.
- Sell the program. Invite parents to watch classes. Propose and carry out a PTA program highlighting the skills and sequences children learn. When parents see a good educational program, they are likely to support it.

Planning

Chapter 3 contains an overview of the content that can be developed through the learning experiences in chapters 6 to 10. An important decision you must make as a teacher is how much of the content described in this book to use in your program. Remember, this is only one of five books (Belka, 1994; Buschner, 1994; Purcell, 1994; and Ratliffe & Ratliffe, 1994) that describe the content of physical education for children. Ideally, your program will include content from each of the areas, so you have some difficult decisions to make. A complete outline for planning is provided in *Teaching Children Physical Education* (Graham, 1992), but only you can develop the plans that will work best at your school. Also included here in this book are those benchmarks (Franck et al., 1991) that relate specifically to the content area of gymnastics. Use these benchmarks to help decide which aspects of the content are most important for your children to learn (see Figure 1.5).

Where to start in gymnastics and what sequence to follow is really a matter of personal preference. With preschool and kindergarten gymnastics, large groups or whole-class instruction works well for short periods, much the same as the opening circle or story time works in the classroom. Having an opening activity in which everyone participates is a good routine, providing the regularity that gives children the confidence and security they need to be successful in the gymnasium. Most of the time very young children spend in gymnastics should be structured for small groups or individual work. A thematic learning environment, created as one of several learning centers that children can choose to visit as interest comes and goes, would be helpful. For example, set out mats with hoops in vertical or horizontal alignment and ask the children to find different ways to go over and under them or in and out as a theme for the day. Another theme could be setting up mats and benches to use in exploring different ways to move forward and backward. Have the children try different ways of moving on the hands and feet. Over time you can structure learning centers to ensure that children explore and develop movement patterns based on body awareness, space awareness, effort actions, and relationships (BSER). Although the instruction may not seem formal, young children will learn an incredible amount that prepares them to succeed in later, more formal, schooling.

During the early primary years, children should acquire a sound foundation of traveling actions, balancing skills, and rotation work. They should learn to do all of this work on the floor or a mat by themselves. Good body management is essential. Develop good control and efficient movement. Design sequences that progress in a developmentally appropriate way. Build on the children's successes. As it is appropriate, add equipment like boxes and benches, hoops, ropes, and hurdles. In the intermediate years children progress toward more difficult skills, so add larger equipment, introduce partner work, and develop more formal, complicated sequences.

Another important planning factor is the length of time you have taught the children. Your plans will (and should) be different for the first year of a program than for the tenth year. When you have worked with fifth or sixth graders from the time they started school, they will be able to do, and will know, different things than the fifth and sixth graders did your first year at that school.

Safety Guidelines and Liability

Gymnastics teachers are always concerned about providing a safe learning environment for children (see Figure 2.4). No one would want to place children in an unsafe situation where they might get hurt. Teachers should consider these guidelines to provide a safe environment.

- Teach the children a safe protocol on how to use the equipment. What activities are acceptable on a given piece of equipment? Injuries usually occur when equipment is misused.
- Gymnastics should be conducted in a work-like environment. What is acceptable behavior? Many injuries occur when kids are fooling around, goofing off, or daring each other.
- Practice a skill first on the floor and then close to the floor on a wide base, before taking it to a more difficult level. Mastery is the key.
- Provide enough room for children to move safely. In small areas like classrooms, stages, and hallways, space is a critical issue. Make sure there is enough room to complete a skill without bumping a wall, another child, or a piece of equipment. For example, roll from near a wall toward an open space. Cartwheel lengthwise if the space is long and narrow.
- Provide a safe surface. Mats should be placed under and beside any large apparatus for proper padding. On an outdoor surface use mats or large parachutes to protect children's skin and clothes. Remove all glass and sharp objects from the area.
- Inspect each apparatus regularly as a safety precaution. Is the surface free of splinters? Tighten any loose nuts or bolts, and remove protruding items such as nuts, bolts, dollies, and transporters.
- Make sure each piece of equipment is stable and set up on a nonskid surface. Equipment should not move in use.

Occasionally a bad accident in gymnastics has occurred, and the school district has barred the use of a specific piece of equipment or even the

Figure 2.4   Providing a safe learning environment is always important in gymnastics. Students can spot each other when necessary, or the teacher can spot for them.

teaching of gymnastics. Any accident is unfortunate, and the job of reinstituting a full-blown gymnastics program into the school may be difficult. However, it is not impossible. Collect good literature on the benefits of gymnastics for children and present it to the principal, superintendent, or school board. Sell the program by developing safety measures and body management. Develop a program based on sound tumbling skills on the floor and through the use of wide benches and boxes close to the floor, perhaps naming it body management instead of gymnastics.

Along with safety, teachers are always concerned with liability. The best protection is teaching well. Teach sound skills, good body mechanics, and proper progressions. It is also prudent to have good liability insurance. Teachers should enroll in a plan that affords adequate protection ($100,000 to $1 million). Riders on home-owner's insurance and liability plans sold through education associations (NEA, AAHPERD) offer reasonable insurance.

Summary

One of the most valid criticisms of physical education programs has been that they were designed only for athletes—and were a painful experience for those who were poorly skilled. Contemporary physical educators are moving away from this one-model-fits-all pattern of restrictive physical education toward programs that are adjusted, adapted, and designed specifically to match the abilities, interests, and needs of individual children. This chapter describes some of the considerations that contemporary teachers take into account when designing programs specifically for the children at their school.

Chapter 3

Incorporating Gymnastics Into Your Program

The content areas of games, dance, and gymnastics include many skills. Rather than consider skills individually, it is convenient to group them into categories that can organize units of work. With gymnastics there are several ways to organize such frameworks. Some educators group gymnastics into stunts, tumbling, and apparatus. Others organize it around a framework of manipulative, stability, and locomotor actions. Still other teachers use as frameworks body, space, effort, and relationships concepts.

In developing the content for this book, I have selected skill themes as the framework. Three skill themes form the framework: the body's traveling actions, static work, and rotation (Figure 3.1).

Each skill theme can be thought of as a *set*, or group of activities, as in mathematics. Traveling actions include activities in which the focus or intent is to move the body from one place to another. Static work includes those activities in which the focus or intent is to achieve stillness or balance. Rotation includes activities in which there is a focus or intent to twist, turn, or roll around one of the three axes of the body.

As is evident in Figure 3.1, each of the skill themes can function as a separate set. As these sets of skill themes interact with each other, overlapping and joining of the themes occurs. This intersection and union of sets is a mathematical concept that is useful in looking at

gymnastics work. For example, skills, such as rolling, at times might be thought of as turning around the body's horizontal or vertical axis. At other times a rolling action may function to transfer the body weight from one place to another as a traveling action. While traveling through the air, a gymnast might twist, turn, or rotate the body to create a particular shape or change directions.

In many instances one skill set will be the main theme for a given lesson, although other skills will support, link, or combine with the main theme to unify gymnastics work.

The beauty of thinking about gymnastics as sets, or units of work, is that we can at times

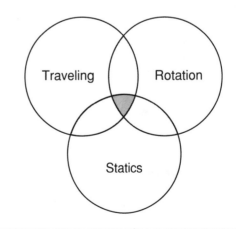

Figure 3.1 Skill themes for gymnastics.

21

separate out single skills to teach developmentally by refining and extending tasks. Using sets of skills also allows us to combine work logically. In reality, we associate gymnastics floor exercise, the balance beam, or parallel bars with routines. Gymnasts continually strive to perfect individual skills and then combine them with others to develop sequences or routines. They piece actions together, or link one action to another, to use the momentum created by one action flowing into the next. This flow, this functional movement with complete body awareness and management, is what makes gymnastics aesthetic.

Traveling Actions

Traveling actions of the body in this book are intended to include all work in which the focus is to move the body from one place to another (see Table 3.1). The intent of some traveling actions is to move the body to a new position on the floor or over a distance with reference to equipment. The intent of other traveling actions is to shift or transfer the body's weight to a new position, thus moving only a very short distance. Several major categories of traveling actions exist.

Steplike Travel Using the Feet

All of the steplike actions of the feet are traveling. As we transfer weight from one foot to the other (walk, run, leap), from one foot to the same (hop), from two feet to two feet (jump), and from two feet to one foot or one foot to two feet, traveling occurs. These basic stepping actions in combination produce skipping, galloping, sliding, and other more innovative ways of using the feet to travel across the floor. (Refer to Buschner, 1994, for more specific information.) The use of the feet to produce traveling is called locomotion.

Steplike Travel Using the Hands, Feet, and Knees

Steplike actions also occur when one uses the hands and feet or hands and knees to travel. Some gymnastics teachers include these types of steplike actions within a category of weight transfer, but in this book I have chosen to separate them. When young children explore what their bodies can do to travel through space, they learn crawling, the bear walk, the crab walk, bunny hop, animal walks of other sorts, the coffee grinder, and other stuntlike movements. These movement tasks, whether taught directly or indirectly (by challenging children to find different ways to move with their hands and feet), help children develop strength in the arms and legs and gain confidence in managing their body.

In this book, the words *gymnast* and *gymnastics-like* are used to set a tone, to establish a philosophy, or set a frame of mind for teachers and children. Gymnastics is different from games and dance: It includes basic body management skills as well as more formal gymnastics skills. This means that not everything is acceptable under the rubric of gymnastics. As children think like gymnasts, they will work more productively to link actions and skills into sequences and routines reflecting this attitude. What is *not* gymnastics-like are uncontrolled attempts at animal walks, silly sounds, racing about, and relays. To encourage the development of a gymnastics philosophy or attitude, always think of children as gymnasts.

As children develop these beginning skills using their hands and feet to transfer weight, consider the question of what work is gymnastics-like. What type of work in this category would you wish to continue and encourage, and what type would you try to eliminate? Beyond the early primary years crawling, simple animal walks, and the like should be discouraged: They are no longer useful. They lead nowhere and are not gymnastics-like. As children develop readiness skills, arm and shoulder strength, and confidence, their steplike traveling gymnastics should

Table 3.1   Traveling Actions of the Body

Steplike— using feet	Steplike— using hands, feet, knees	Weight transfer	Flight
Walk	Crawl	Rocking,	Takeoff
Run	Bear walk	rolling	Suspension
Hop	Crab walk	Twisting,	Landing
Jump	Bunny-hop	turning	Trampette
Skip	Mule kick	Sliding	work
Gallop	Coffee grinder		Vaulting
Slide	Walkover—		
Leap	front, back		
	Wheeling		
	(cartwheel,		
	roundoff)		
	Springing (front		
	and back		
	handspring)		

include wheeling actions (the cartwheel or round-off), springing actions (the front or back handspring), and other actions in which weight is transferred from the feet to the hands and back to the feet. They might practice the walkover, or use the hands to transfer weight over a bench, box, or horse.

Weight Transfer

The category of weight transfer as a traveling action includes all the movements that focus on the transfer of weight from one adjacent body part to another. Rocking forward and back on frontal or back body surfaces or from side to side, rolling actions of all types, and sliding are examples of work in this category. While there is some crossover of categories in rolling between traveling and rotation actions, this is not a problem, keeping in mind the idea of unified sets of work. Sometimes the focus of a roll involves principles of rotation. At other times rolling action helps us travel across a mat, arrive at a piece of equipment, or move off a piece of equipment to link with the next part in a sequence.

Twisting and turning actions of all types can also help the body travel a short distance and transfer body weight from one position to another. A person in a V-seat, with weight back on the hands, might effectively turn halfway over to the right or left into a push-up position. Another person might twist out of a shoulder stand to a position on two knees or a knee and a foot.

Sliding in this category is not to be confused with sliding sideways on the feet. Sliding, as a means of weight transfer, is a shift of body weight from one position to another by choosing a particular body surface along which to slide. For example, a child lying on her stomach on the floor or a bench might anchor the hands and slide along her stomach or shins into a push-up or front support position. Someone might slide on the stomach over a horse, take weight on the hands, and finish with a roll to the feet. From a push-up position, a person could put his head on the floor, slide the feet toward his hands into a pike position, and press up into a headstand. In each instance the sliding action helped transfer body weight and was a functional part of the sequence.

Flight

Flight, the last category of traveling actions, includes such movements as the takeoff, suspension, or travel through the air, and landing. Initial attempts at takeoff are exploratory in nature and should include steplike actions of the feet. Over time, children should learn specialized forms of the takeoff leading to vaulting, such as the step into the two foot hurdle action used in diving and vaulting in gymnastics. During the flight phase of the jump the focus is on the body's shape—wide, narrow; extended, tucked; symmetrical, asymmetrical, and so on. Landings usually should be on the feet and controlled. Soft, squishy landings are key, in which children learn to absorb their body weight smoothly by giving with the knees. More advanced students may learn landings on the hands, such as a dive roll, or even on other body parts; the principles are always the same. To receive weight, the body must give, or absorb the landing smoothly, under control.

Initial work on flight should be on the floor. Gradually takeoffs and landings can be from raised surfaces, such as jumping onto and off of boxes and benches. As children gain skill and confidence, you can introduce special pieces of equipment, such as Reuter boards and trampettes, to emphasize the flight phase of the jump.

Static Work

Gymnastics work within the skill theme of statics includes those activities in which the focus or intent is to achieve stillness or balance (see Table 3.2). Initially, you are trying to help children achieve stillness in a controlled manner. Activities such as running and then stopping or freezing can help children differentiate between movement and no movement. They need to learn to feel the tightness or tension of the muscles

Table 3.2   Static Characteristics of the Body

Characteristics of balance	Principles of balance	Types of balance
Moments of stillness	Base of support	Upright or inverted
Tightness of body	Center of gravity	Symmetrical or asymmetrical
Control	Counter-tension/ counterbalance	Hanging
	Linking actions	Supporting
	Movement into and out of balance	Relationship to equipment
		Individual or partner

held in a static position. After learning to gain stillness on the feet, students may shift to creating balances on other body parts in a controlled manner. Emphasize control by counting to 3 or 5. During early balance experiences counting is helpful to focus on mastery, but it should gradually receive less emphasis. In reality, gymnasts performing routines rarely hold positions for long periods of time. Balance positions are held just long enough to show control—almost as if to say, I could stay here longer if I wanted to. The real beauty of gymnastics is not in the static balances but in the flow created when a gymnast links movements to and from those balances into a sequence or routine.

Principles of Balance

The main principles that govern balance stem from the base of support and center of gravity (see Figure 3.2). In general, a wide base of support, with several body parts acting as bases, will be more stable than a narrow base with fewer body parts serving as supports. A low center of gravity is more stable than a high one. A key to choosing good balance positions is to keep the center of gravity over the base of support. Then align the body parts that serve as bases. In a headstand the head and hands must form a triangle, and the head and arms must distribute weight equally, with the hips and legs directly over the base to create a vertical column from the spine through the extended legs and feet. When the legs serve as a base, the knees and hips should be in vertical alignment with the feet. Good alignment produces strong balances.

At times a gymnast chooses to use the concepts of counterbalance and counter-tension to assume positions of balance (see Figure 3.3). In a *counterbalance position* the gymnast's center of gravity is outside the base of support, but by pushing against another gymnast or supporting one's weight with or against a piece of equipment, a stable balance position is achieved. In a *counter-tension balance position* two or more gymnasts are pulling away from each other with their center of gravity outside their base, but because they are countering each other's force in opposite directions through tension, a stable balance is achieved.

A gymnast may also use the concept of balance as a means to move into, out of, or from one balance position to another. When balancing in a given position, such as a scale, a gymnast might take the trunk forward and one leg back. He or she could extend the arms sideways parallel to the floor for more stability. As long as the center of gravity remains over the support leg, the balance will be stable. Yet, by experimenting with a lean forward, backward, or sideways, a gymnast can find the point where loss of balance occurs. Once this loss of balance occurs, a gymnast can use the momentum generated to carry the body smoothly into the next balance. A twist, turn, roll, step, or other body action used under control is the common method of linking balances into sequences. Gymnasts continually seek ways to link balances smoothly and with control through actions of counterbalance: balance, then loss of balance, then balance regained. No falls. No crashes. No glitches. No unwanted or unnecessary steps. Gymnasts want the controlled use of momentum into and out of balances.

Types of Balance

Gymnastics includes many types of balance. Balances may be thought of as *upright*, with the

Figure 3.2   Examples of balances with good bases and alignment.

Counterbalance   Counter-tension   Counterbalance

Figure 3.3   Examples of counterbalance and counter-tension with partners and equipment.

head higher than the hips, or *inverted*, with the head lower than the hips. Balance positions may be *symmetrical* or *asymmetrical*. In symmetrical balances the left and right sides of the body mirror each other, or are the same. The headstand, handstand, V-seat, and other common balances are symmetrical. By changing one arm or leg position to a bend, stretch, or twist, thereby making the left side different from the right, one assumes an asymmetrical balance. There are countless variations of asymmetrical balances. Considered within the BSER framework, symmetrical and asymmetrical balances both are types of body shapes among the process variables.

With the introduction of equipment such as a bench, box, beam, bar, or jungle gym a gymnast can create still other balances from hanging or support positions. Additional relationships to equipment occur as gymnasts create balance positions, supporting their weight completely or partially on the equipment. Balances can be done individually or with a partner or small group.

Rotation Actions

Rotary movement occurs around the three axes of the body: that is, the three planes (dimensions) of space. These are the vertical (longitudinal), horizontal, and transverse (medial) axes. If a rod were placed vertically from head to toe, rotation would occur in a vertical plane. Jumps with quarter, half, and full turns in the air and pencil

rolls or log rolls are typical of rotation around a vertical axis. A rod placed horizontally from hip to hip (side to side) would allow for rotation around a horizontal axis. Forward rolls, backward rolls, somersaults, and front and back handsprings are typical examples of rotation around a horizontal axis. Front and back hip circles are examples of horizontal rotation when using equipment. A rod placed horizontally (front to back) would allow for rotation around a transverse axis. Wheeling actions such as a cartwheel or roundoff, on the floor and onto and off of equipment, are typical of rotation around a transverse axis.

Principles of Rotation

Rotation work in gymnastics includes twisting, turning, or rolling activities around one of the body's three axes (see Table 3.3). Movement around these three axes of the body is influenced by certain mechanical principles. The *rate* of rotation around a fixed point or axis increases as the radius (distance from axis to end point) decreases. Conversely, the rate of rotation around a fixed point or axis is decreased if the radius is increased. This concept is important for gymnasts, divers, skaters, and other athletes who use turns and rolls in their sport. Staying tucked in a forward roll, hip circle, or somersault will help athletes spin quickly. It shortens or decreases the radius. Opening up or extending away from the center will slow or stop the rate

Table 3.3   Rotary Actions of the Body

Principles of rotation	Movement around three axes	Rotation of body
Radius of rotation	Vertical	In space
Eye focus	Spins	Around
	Turns	equipment
	Pencil or log rolls	
	Horizontal	
	Forward rolls	
	Backward rolls	
	Handsprings	
	Somersaults	
	Hip circles	
	Transverse	
	Cartwheels/wheeling	
	Roundoffs/springing	

of rotation: It lengthens or increases the radius. Gymnasts can use this principle to their advantage when they wish to accelerate, or speed up a movement, and to decelerate, or slow a movement. For example, gymnasts doing a headstand or handstand into a forward roll and finishing in a standing position would stay long, or extended, to begin the turn and generate momentum. They would then lower the body and quickly tuck, using that speed to complete the roll to the feet. Finally they would stand and extend to slow the action and stop the momentum. Think long and tall, short and small, long and tall.

Learning to fixate the eyes on a stationary point is another helpful concept or principle for any athlete who turns, rolls, or spins about. Maintaining eye contact with a fixed spot gives a reference point where the body is in space. Using this principle helps gymnasts maintain balance and overcome any tendencies toward dizziness.

Rotation of the Body

Rotation in space occurs when the body moves around any of its three axes without equipment being involved, such as rolling actions on the mat, sitting spins, cartwheels, roundoffs, springing actions, and jump-turns in the air. Rotation around equipment occurs when a bar, beam, bench, or other piece of equipment acts as the radius of rotation.

Process Variables

Each of these skill themes involves a continual awareness of body, space, effort, and relationships

(BSER) concepts (see Table 3.4). Rudolf Laban originally developed these *process variables* to provide a framework for dance. Superimposing Laban's process variables onto the travel, static, and rotation skill themes provides a useful gymnastics movement vocabulary for students of all ages and skill levels. Each of these process variables can be interwoven with learning experiences on the skill themes of traveling, statics, and rotation at appropriate times. Although each is important in itself, they will become subthemes as I discuss the main skill themes.

Body

Focus for a moment on the body and what it can do: actions of the whole body and of specific body parts, activities of the body, and shapes that the body can assume. Actions of the body include curling, bending, twisting, and swinging movements. Actions of specific body parts include supporting weight, leading a movement, receiving force (or weight), and giving force. The body's activities include locomotion, nonlocomotion, and manipulation. In this book the traveling actions are locomotor activities, and static work is the equivalent in nonlocomotor activities. Manipulative activities are part of rhythmic gymnastics, but the skill themes of throwing, catching, and kicking (manipulative actions) lie outside the realm of this book (see Belka, 1994 and Buschner, 1994). Finally, the body can assume such shapes as angular, straight, round, twisted, symmetrical, and asymmetrical.

Space

Directions, pathways, levels, planes, and extensions are the spatial elements gymnasts use most. Traveling and rotation skills move the body in forward, backward, sideways, up and down, and diagonal directions. By selecting a pathway in which to perform a sequence of actions, children can link together appropriate floor or air patterns for body movement. For example, "Jump, roll, then travel, taking weight on the hands" may lead to a zigzag, straight, circular, or twisted pathway. Practicing along straight lines during floor work helps children to transfer the skills and sequences later onto benches and beam.

Although in traveling and rotation the body moves through *general space*, static work stays within one's *personal space*. The body can be held or moved through a range of *levels* from very low to very high. Incorporating level changes into a

Table 3.4 BSER Framework of Human Movement

Body (what the body does)	Space (where the body moves)	Effort (how the body performs the movement)	Relationships (relationships that occur in movement)
Actions of the body	Areas	Time	Body parts
Curl	General	Fast, accelerating, sudden	Above, below
Bend	Personal	Slow, decelerating, sustained	Apart, together
Twist	Directions	Force (weight)	Behind, in front of
Swing	Forward	Firm, strong	Meeting, parting
Actions of body parts	Backward	Fine, light	Near, far
Support body weight	Sideward	Space	Individuals and groups
Lead action	Upward	Direct, straight	Mirroring, matching
Receive weight/force	Downward	Indirect, flexible	Contrasting
Apply force	Diagonal	Flow	Successive, alternating
Activities of the body	Levels	Bound, stoppable, jerky	Questioning, answering
Locomotor	Low	Free, ongoing, smooth	Acting, reacting
Nonlocomotor	Medium		Leading, following
Manipulative	High		Lifting, being lifted
Body shapes	Pathways		Supporting, being supported
Angular	Straight		Apparatus and equipment
Straight	Curved		Around, along
Round	Zigzag		Over, under
Twisted	Twisted		Near, far
Symmetrical, asymmetrical	Planes		Above, below, alongside
	Wheel, sagittal		Arriving on, dismounting
	Door, frontal		Other types
	Table, horizontal		Goals, boundaries
	Extensions		Music, sounds
	Large		Poems, stories, words
	Small		Beats, patterns
			Art, artifacts

sequence of actions gives a student the opportunity to create responses with more variety and aesthetic appeal. Changes in levels also apply to body parts in relation to each other. For example, requesting students to make a balance in which their feet are at a higher level than their hands may result in a shoulder balance, headstand, or even a handstand.

The planes of space define the three dimensions of space, much the same as do the three axes of rotation. The *table* or *horizontal plane* divides top from bottom. The *door* or *frontal plane* divides left from right. The *wheel* or *sagittal plane* divides front from back. Think of movement or balance positions as taking place in one or more of the planes of space. A headstand going from low to high takes place primarily in the horizontal plane. Sliding sideways on the feet across a bench emphasizes movement in the frontal plane. Movement of the body forward and then backward emphasizes the sagittal plane.

Spatial extensions of large and small occur during gymnastics when the body is extended, or body parts are far from the center, and when the body is flexed, or body parts are close to the center. A second kind of extension occurs when a sequence takes a gymnast far away from a point of origin, covering a lot of space, or keeps the gymnast close to the point of origin.

Effort

Effort qualities consist of time, space, weight (or force), and flow. *Time* qualifies movement as occurring very quickly or in a slow, sustained fashion. A roll or a steplike traveling action may be executed quickly or slowly. Pressing up into a headstand might occur slowly, in a very controlled manner, and a roll out of a headstand might be done quickly to establish the momentum to move into the next action.

The variable of *space* refers to direct and indirect movement. A gymnast moving across the floor or moving to arrive at a piece of equipment may choose to travel directly to a chosen place or use an indirect pathway, such as a zigzag or curved pathway. As the arms, legs, or other body parts move through the air they also move directly or indirectly through space.

The concept of *weight* or *force* refers to the amount of energy given to an action. Some gymnastics actions are soft and light; others require an extraordinary amount of heavy force. Skipping across the floor or hopping along a bench might be soft and delicate. A vaulting action or press into a handstand could use a lot of force.

Flow refers to whether a movement is free and smooth or bound and stoppable. Turning or spinning actions (rotation) are often free and flowing, whereas the balancing actions of static work are often bound and tense. Each of these effort qualities, although described separately, often interacts in combination with other(s). Running across the floor may be quick, light, direct, and flowing. Balancing in a V-seat on a bench might be sustained, forceful, and bound. (For further information on the effort qualities of movement see Buschner, 1994).

Relationships

Relationships involve interactions between body parts, between one person and another, between one person and a group, or between a person and equipment. Some of the relationships among body parts are above and below, apart and together, behind and in front, meeting and parting, and near and far. Working with a partner or small group, an individual may lead or follow; mirror, match, or contrast; lift or be lifted; and support or be supported. Within groups, we use the term *successive* to refer to an ordering (1, 2, 3) or taking turns in a small group and *alternating* to refer to taking turns in a partnership (you move, I move). Terms such as questioning and answering or acting and reacting are used mostly by dancers as they relate and interpret their expressive movements.

Working with equipment, whether large or small, a gymnast may move around, alongside, over, under, above, or below the apparatus. Gymnasts also move to arrive on the apparatus or to dismount the apparatus as well as moving near and far from the equipment. Music or sounds may accompany a gymnast who would design movement in a sequence to relate to the music. (Other types of relationships in the BSER framework are used with reference to games [goals, boundaries] and dance [poems, stories, words, beats, patterns, art, and artifacts].) Any of these general relationships can combine with the skill themes of traveling, statics, and rotation.

Summary

I have organized this book around the three skill themes of traveling, statics, and rotation. Each work unit (main skill theme) or chapter is further subdivided into lessons that use representative subsets, skills, or ideas. Laban's process variables of body, space, effort, and relationships support the development of content at both the unit and lesson plan level.

Unlike earlier books on gymnastics, which emphasize a single stunt or skill for a lesson (e.g., the forward roll or cartwheel) or a specific Laban theme (use of space, shape, time), my emphasis in skill theme work is on linking actions or the transitions that flow from one action to another.

Chapter 4

Principles for Teaching Gymnastics

In developing a gymnastics program, teachers should have a set of principles that guide and direct their decisions. Some of the principles might relate directly to the *Developmentally Appropriate Physical Education Practices for Children* (Council on Physical Education for Children, 1992). While I cannot cover all circumstances, the principles should provide a sound basis for decisions about developing a sound program in body management.

Equipment Provisions

Many physical educators equate gymnastics with an elaborate inventory of commercial equipment (i.e., vaulting boxes, parallel bars, balance beams); consequently, they consider a lack of such equipment justification to exclude gymnastics from the program. These notions must be challenged. Body management skills can be readily practiced and refined using mats, wooden benches—and a little resourcefulness. For example, skipping ropes, carpet squares, hula hoops, hurdles made from paper wands, and milk crates (common in most schools), along with mats and benches, are sufficient apparatus to motivate and challenge students (see Figure 4.1).

With this simple equipment students can travel, balance, and rotate on, over, in, out,
under, along, and beside the apparatus: These tasks, in turn, help children practice linking actions. They can learn to form a continuous sequence, an important component in body management.

The key principles in using equipment are modification and innovation. Keeping in mind the skill themes of traveling, statics, and rotation, the teacher decides which specific skills children will practice and learn in sequence or linked together. These skills may be balancing, hanging, supporting, rolling, or steplike actions. After deciding to develop a particular skill theme, a teacher considers what type of equipment might be useful and how to arrange it to enhance skill development in the particular area. If balancing is the chosen area, a teacher then decides whether balancing will be done on the floor or on equipment.

What equipment is available on which to balance? You may be blessed with commercial 10' × 12" benches or nice vaulting boxes. Chances are, however, that you do not have enough benches and boxes to permit one piece for every one or two children. The focus of this gymnastics work is body management, however, and not the development of competitive Olympic gymnastics. Feeling encouraged to innovate and modify, you ask yourself what is readily available for balance. Perhaps you will come up with tables, chairs,

Figure 4.1   Although some programs may have standard gymnastics equipment, you can also use boxes, benches, and chairs as equipment.

milk crates, folded mats, or cardboard boxes filled with newspaper, all acceptable surfaces on which children can safely balance.

In addition to using innovative objects such as tables and chairs for gymnastics purposes, you can creatively modify the gymnastics apparatus you do have to develop body management skills (see Figure 4.2). For example, children can do forward hip circles around a balance beam or a singular parallel bar. They can work under a balance beam performing rolling actions, balance against the beam, hang under it, and rise up from the beam. Students can use vaulting horses

Figure 4.2   Equipment can be used in innovative ways.

to support body weight or create balance shapes, and slide off of them.

The arrangement of equipment is another key to successfully linking gymnastics actions together and developing sequence work. A mat placed at the end of or beside a bench can mark points of entry and exit. Placing the mat between a bench and the parallel bars encourages linking actions between these apparatuses. A teacher first decides which skills to link or sequence and then arranges the equipment accordingly.

Safety Concerns

Many public school administrators and physical educators hesitate to teach gymnastics because of their concern for legal liability and safety. Like other risk sports, such as rock climbing, whitewater canoeing or kayaking, gymnastics presents challenge and with it some danger. That does not mean these sports should not be taught. When care is exercised to use good equipment and sound educational practices, risk sports have very good records for safety.

In promoting a strong body management program in gymnastics, teachers' concerns for safety should turn primarily to the areas of equipment and educational practice. Select equipment on the basis of quality. Mats should be durable and absorbent. Such large equipment as balance beams, benches, boxes, and bars should meet standards set by the industry. If tables, chairs, milk crates and other multi-purpose equipment are used, inspect each piece for sturdiness and carefully decide how to work with a given piece. Always monitor equipment to make sure it is suitable. Equipment should be placed judiciously, leaving adequate room between pieces to permit the intended actions. As a rule, mats should be placed beside or under equipment to provide absorbent landings and to cushion any falls which may occur.

The clothing children wear and whether they should wear shoes are part of equipment considerations. Clothes should be loose enough to permit free, unrestricted movement, but not so baggy as to risk catching on something. Gym uniforms and nylon, stretch lycra clothing intended for active movement are probably the best. Indoors, I recommend that children go barefoot. Gymnasts have a much better feel for the floor and supporting surface when the feet or skin directly contact the floor or equipment. Tactile-kinesthetic perception is more acute, giving the gymnast important messages about the body and space. Outdoors, non-skid shoes are acceptable for safety.

Besides selecting and using equipment well, teaching must be based on other sound principles. Spotting, a primary concern, is a technique used to provide the gymnast assistance in executing a skill. Another student or the teacher usually is in position to help at the critical time in the skill's performance. While direct assistance is not always given, the spotter is there if needed for safety purposes. Olympic gymnastics programs typically use spotting. In this book, I advocate spotting only in selected circumstances (see Figure 4.3). In general, spotting is used for developing new and more difficult skills and for combining previously learned skills. Use it on an individual basis, as children need or request it. A program in body management teaches children to move under control.

It is important not to permit crashing, silly off-task behavior, or foolish, daredevil tricks. Make sure children have mastered a skill at an easier level before allowing them to attempt it at a higher level. A child should not attempt an actual handstand before having control over taking weight on the hands and coming down softly on the feet. Gradually a student will kick higher and get vertical alignment under control. Teach children to recover from any loss of control by twisting out into a cartwheel or tucking into a forward roll. With rolling, a child who controls a

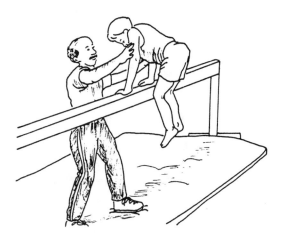

Figure 4.3 Use spotting when developing new and more difficult skills.

roll on the floor next may try to roll onto, along, or off equipment. The environment should be specially set for these occasions: Use extra raised or folded mats to reduce any possible fall. Only those children who have mastered easier skills should be encouraged to perform them in a more challenging situation. All children should work within the limits of their ability. You can reduce risks by not requiring that all children try a given skill, instead allowing them to modify actions within a movement challenge.

Let's imagine an example when a task is set and children are working, perhaps at transferring their weight from the feet to hands and back to the feet. As the teacher you observe for skill level and may call a few children over for specific instruction and spotting on a back walkover, front handspring or back handspring. It is not important that everyone master these more advanced skills. Perhaps a child is working on a sequence, combining two skills, or trying to perform a skill in a new way or on a new piece of equipment. The child should feel free to ask for help (spotting) in these situations. Encourage children to take self-responsibility, to work within their ability level, and to develop movement based on sound mechanical principles.

Children's Ability Level and Rate of Learning

Children enter gymnastics classes at different sizes, shapes, and ability levels. They come from different backgrounds and with varied experiences. These differences are evident even in the early grades (see Figure 4.4). For some youngsters, gymnastics is natural. Their parents have been doing gymnastics-like activities with them, such as rolling on the floor and tossing them in the air, since they were toddlers. They may already have had a variety of experiences in a pre-school tumbling program. Other children may not have had this experience, but are blessed with the right kind of bodies. They are small, strong, and flexible. Some students will have all of the tools, but be attracted to spectator sports or no sports at all because the family does not encourage active participation. A few simply are not gifted in gymnastics. Many of these children are large, verging on obesity. They may have the desire to participate, yet lack the strength, flexibility, and body coordination. Perhaps they lack desire because they are embarrassed or self-conscious. They do not want to make fools of themselves in front of others. With older children these differences often escalate. Some go on to become accomplished gymnasts, even Olympic gymnasts. Others may not progress at all, finding it difficult to control a forward roll or cartwheel.

All of these children enter our gymnastics classes. As teachers we should keep in mind these differences in ability and rate of learning. Unlike Olympic gymnastics, which is primarily sensitive to content progressions from easy to more difficult, a system of body management should encompass individual needs. We need to be sensitive to and knowledgeable of how able children are. We need to understand content progressions, from easy to difficult, to modify and adapt tasks suitably to meet each child's needs.

Ample Practice

Children need time to practice new skills and to combine skills into sequences, both to gain mastery and develop feelings of success. You might question how to judge how many practice trials are enough. There is no specific number of practice attempts it takes to be sufficient. Every child is different: Some take longer than others. Certainly, just as no one learns to throw or dribble a ball, or perform a dance, in only a few tries, we cannot expect most people to learn gymnastics skills well with relatively few trials.

A given lesson should provide 10 to 20 appropriate practice tries for each specific task. Creating that many practice opportunities in varied ways dictates how we organize a lesson. It is not efficient to have one line with the teacher spotting every child at every trial. One long relay line makes for very few practice attempts. Even having two to four gymnastics stations for a class of 30 children with students rotating, would place 8 to 10 youngsters at each station. A child would have only one turn and then wait for seven to nine others to complete their turns. In a typical 30-minute lesson this arrangement would allow only two to three trials at each station: That is not enough practice for mastery.

We must organize the lessons and provide enough equipment to allow children to work as individuals, in partnerships, or in small groups of three to four. With that low ratio children are guaranteed more practice time and less waiting time (see Figure 4.5).

Figure 4.4   Children should progress at their own rates and levels.

Figure 4.5 Children should have ample opportunities for practice.

Give a realistic look at how many tasks can be presented in a given lesson: In order to increase practice time, you will have to decrease instruction time. Using a goal of 10 to 20 practice trials for each task, there probably should be no more than three to six tasks in a lesson (i.e., 3 tasks could be practiced 20 times or 6 tasks practiced 10 times each). That averages out to two practice attempts every minute, including instruction and waiting. By keeping instructions short, clear, and succinct, we can accomplish this goal.

Children profit from repetition. To prevent boredom, change tasks slightly within or at least between lessons. For example, if static work is the focus of the lesson and children are balancing on different bases of support, you might refine the work by making the children aware of extensions through the arms and legs or smooth curved lines through the back. A task could be varied by having children alter the height, relationship of the body parts, or shape of their balances. Likewise, a sequence can be changed slightly to produce a new focus. Add a roll to the balance-travel-balance sequence. Require one of the balances in the sequence to be on a piece of equipment. In each instance, the children have a new focus or challenge. They will stay on-task and profit from variety in their practice.

Direct and Indirect Teaching Styles

As teachers we sometimes want to be very specific in what we assign children to learn. This is a good way to build skill and develop sound fundamentals. It gives children a solid foundation from which to build. This type of teaching style has been called direct, invariant, or command-oriented (Graham, 1992). In direct teaching a specific skill or routine is presented. The teacher sets a standard of performance. Children attempt to conform to the standard, having little or no choice. Although this approach may work well in a formal Olympic gymnastics setting, which takes successful performers to ever higher levels of progressive skills, it does not work well in a system that fosters body management. It may doom some children to failure and stifle creativity and thinking.

For gymnastics with children I would promote a more indirect teaching style, one that is oriented to discovery, questioning, and problem solving (Figure 4.6). At times it is appropriate to teach specific skills, principles for good body mechanics, and movement fundamentals or concepts directly. These aspects serve as a foundation, or set of building blocks, from which children can begin to make choices. In this book you will find ways to teach children about traveling, balancing, and rotating from a conceptual point of view. Children first learn the fundamental principles of traveling, balancing, and rotating, and then are asked to make choices: Combine two steplike traveling actions; balance your body in a stretched, then curled shape; sequence a travel, balance, and a roll.

A teacher could easily say skip, then hop, or balance in a T-position, then curl into a ball. Ultimately, is it more valuable to the child to copy the teacher, parrot-like, or become empowered to make decisions and create resolution to a movement problem? I contend that encouraging children to make movement decisions gives them ownership of the material. They may work at their own level of ability. They are

Figure 4.6   Indirect teaching encourages children to solve movement problems.

allowed to sequence work in their own unique ways.

Designing Gymnastic Sequences

Sequences help children integrate skills from each of the three main themes and should be used on an informal, developmental basis in every lesson. Occasionally, such as at the end of a work unit, sequences may be used for assessment purposes.

As in dance, sequences are process oriented; they have a beginning, middle, and end. They are movement sentences. In beginning and ending positions gymnasts often stand in erect balances that signal control and draw attention. They say, "Watch me," or "I am finished now." Beginning and ending shapes also can easily draw on other body shapes. During the middle of a sequence or routine, children are given options involving skills from the main themes of traveling, balance, and rotation and from the process variables (BSER). For example, they are told that the sequence must consist of a travel on the feet, a roll, and a symmetrical balance; two rolls using two different body shapes; or three balances at three different levels.

Designing sequences is a good way for teachers to have children consolidate work, reviewing previous movements and adding one new element. All sequence work should focus on and stress good linking actions and transitions from one skill to another. Start sequence work by allowing the children time to explore the possibilities after you state the task. Children need to discover what works at their level, and what doesn't.

Among the many options or choices, the work should next be narrowed to choices the children like or can perform best. At this point, repeat the sequences several times so that children can memorize the sequence, finally performing it without errors.

In the younger grades children should learn simple sequences consisting of three or fewer options. Older children are more able to choose and use additional skills and process variables, developing rather sophisticated pieces of work. The options should be broad or general enough so that all students can develop a sequence, regardless of their skill level.

When to Encourage Student Demonstrations

Many teachers choose only highly skilled students to demonstrate or perform the sequences. As teachers of body management we should think about the purposes of demonstrations and how we choose children to demonstrate. Demonstrations are useful at the beginning of a skill or sequence to present a model or show examples of possibilities (see Figure 4.7). During the middle of a task modelling gives helpful hints and shows how to refine, or expand upon, movement options. Students may correct errors and exhibit work that is on-track (see Graham's description of pinpointing, 1992). Late in the learning process, students demonstrate their sequence work as a performance.

The question remains, whose work to show. In choosing only highly-skilled students, we give children a message with far-reaching implications. The average and below-average students

Figure 4.7 Use demonstrations wisely, as examples of movement possibilities.

begin to feel that we do not value their work. As teachers we should convey that we value the work of all students. By watching all the children for work that is mechanically correct, unique solutions to a movement problem, or hard work that is on-task, we can include everyone at some time in the demonstrations. Catch children in the act of doing something well. Giving everyone an opportunity to be highlighted increases the chances of productive work, since all children know they have an equal chance to be called on.

Keep in mind some other factors in using demonstrations. If one child demonstrates, the rest are watching. It may be useful on occasion to have all the children watch something specific, but it cuts down on activity time. Often it is just as valuable to show work to a partner or small group, or to have each half of the class perform for the rest.

Giving demonstrations makes some children nervous and self-conscious. Children should have the right to decline. Perhaps they do not feel ready or are not at ease with what they are doing. Return to them at a later time.

Accountability— The Gymnastics Work Ethic

Hold children accountable for their actions. You will be just as happy and accepting with a low-skill child performing a seated sideways roll in the sequence as with the advanced learner performing a dive roll over a bench. A child who fools around to cover insecurity or embarrassment is just as dangerous as the irresponsible daredevil showing off. If you set proper rules in the gym-

nasium and enforce them, children will know you mean business: Listen during instruction. Respect others. Take care of equipment. Work productively.

Gymnastics should present a pleasurable, challenging, yet worklike environment. It is serious and not a place to fool around out-of-control. That is how people get hurt. All children should work productively at their ability levels. Like the Army slogan, "Be all that you can be," your attitude should convey that you care and expect their best effort.

Stressing Good Body Mechanics and Aesthetics

With a thematic, or conceptual, approach to teaching, children are given choices as to which skills they perform, how they perform them, and how they link one skill to another in a sequence or routine. It is tempting for teachers to step back and let anything and everything happen. Whatever the child chooses is fine: movement exploration all the way! Unfortunately, that attitude carries risks and is far from what should happen in practice.

While we want children to have choices, as teachers we are the guides and the experts. We recognize good execution and body mechanics. We know what is aesthetically pleasing in gymnastics (see Figure 4.8). It is our job to guide and help children discover proper ways to perform skills and to create flowing transitions between movements. If we see a child rolling forward who needs to push up with the hands at the end of the roll to return to the feet like an elderly person, we

Figure 4.8 Execution and aesthetics are always important in gymnastics.

should step in and teach that student to stay tucked, initiate, and use body momentum. If we see a child placing the hands or head on the floor improperly, we need to teach them a safe way to do it. If we see kids falling and crashing to the floor on their shins, backs, or other body parts, we should teach soft, absorbent landings. For example, when children take weight on the hands and return to the feet, no crashing or falling should occur! Whether children do simple bunny hops or go into handstands, they should always return softly to their feet. Shoulders are always over the hands, with the arms straight and elbows locked.

Furthermore, we should teach children what is aesthetically pleasing (i.e., no saggy bodies; good lines and tension). If the body or a body part is stretched, is it fully extended? If the intent is to curl, does the body or body part become round and smooth? If the intent is to focus attention on line or design, is there commitment to it? Lines can be horizontal, vertical, and so on. Several lines from the arms or legs may be parallel, converge, or diverge. Do they form sharp angles? A gymnast is like an artist painting on a canvas. The gymnast strives to move the body in ways that are not only efficient but also pleasing to the eye. As teachers we can help children make these aesthetic choices.

Summary

As physical educators we continually strive to help children discover ways that work. Where can I go from here? What is the next most logical move? How can I eliminate loss of control, pauses, extra steps, and other glitches? This teaching is difficult because not every child does the same thing. In fact, it would be much easier to create a sequence and just say, do this and that. When you permit every child choices, you must be observant and make suggestions as students need help. Some children discover and latch onto a sequence right away; they need little help except for an occasional comment to polish the work or give it a little flair. Other youngsters will need extensive help and profit from multiple suggestions.

In the final analysis, like an orchestra leader, a teacher is a guide. We should make every effort to know good body mechanics in each of the gymnastics skill themes. We should recognize when work is aesthetically pleasing. Our job is to guide and direct children into discovering proper, pleasing ways to manage their bodies in gymnastics.

Chapter 5

Assessing Children's Progress in Gymnastics

Authentic assessment is a popular concept these days in the educational reform movement. Increasingly, teachers are being held accountable for what children learn or do not learn. As physical educators we must assess children in realistic and meaningful ways that are in the mainstream of acceptable practice.

If we do not design our own ways of assessing children, authorities, such as state education departments or school boards, will select a test battery to administer to our students. The result likely will be a physical fitness test. Although fitness is crucial to the success of a gymnastics program, I do not want it to be the only criterion of assessment. Fitness batteries do not test all of the motor skills children learn in gymnastics, especially neglecting the important cognitive and affective components.

In addition to fitness testing, an authentic measure of children's work in gymnastics should evaluate their skills and their ability to combine skills into sequences, or routines, with smooth transitions. Cognitive development can be assessed verbally or in writing. It should involve the children's knowledge of important cues for particular skills, proper use of mechanical principles, and selection of appropriate process variables (BSER) when they develop movement sequences. Affective development should be reflected in the children's work and the choices they make. Accepting an appropriate level of

challenge, working responsibly, choosing appropriate partners, and working cooperatively are but a few indicators of children's development of good attitudes and values. In this chapter I will develop ideas on how to assess children's gymnastics abilities in each of the three domains: psychomotor, cognitive, and affective.

Realistic Assessment

As pointed out by Graham (1992), many physical educators teach 400 to 600 children a week in an average of two 30-minute lessons. The problems of short class times and large student numbers can make testing seem like an insurmountable task. Yet, there are many reasons to test, including observing each child carefully, assessing the overall program, gaining credibility with administrators and parents, and checking what you, as a teacher, have taught.

Taking into account potential problems with schedules and large class sizes, Graham (1992) suggests ways to save time in administering tests and make testing a valuable experience for children. One such way is to use self- and partner-testing. Children, particularly in the upper elementary grades, can be taught to use checklists (see Figure 5.1) and judge other performers' routines or sequences (see Figure 5.2). As children master particular balancing, traveling, or rotation skills they can place a check by their names.

Directions:

Place a checkmark (✓) across from your name as you can perform each of these skills three times in a row with control and good form. Have a partner check you for control and form.

Name	Seated roll	Pencil roll	Shoulder roll	Forward roll	Backward roll	Roll to two knees	Roll to knee and foot	Roll to two feet	Roll along line	Roll off bench	Roll along bench
1.											
2.											
3.											
4.											
5.											

Figure 5.1   Sample checklist for rolling skills.

They can judge routines or sequences by the inclusion of particular skills or by the inclusion of process variables for qualitative purposes. In a given balance-roll-balance sequence, a partner might learn to check appropriate marks in each box. A Y (yes) or N (no) in the Stillness box would indicate whether balances were controlled for 3 seconds. A "3, 2" in the Base of Support box would indicate that the first balance was on three body parts, and the second was on two body parts. An L, M in the Level box would indicate that the first balance was at a low level, and the second was at a medium level. A simple coding system for each box makes the system workable and a quick scan of the chart would give the teacher immediate feedback on whether the class showed variety in its routines. Giving children responsibility for coding routines would increase their observation skills, develop higher order thinking, and improve aesthetic perception and values, areas in which educational reformers seek improvement.

Assessing every skill or routine for each child in gymnastics is a massive task for one individual teacher. Fortunately, there are other ways to accomplish realistic assessment. You can recruit parents, classroom teachers, high school or university students, or retired volunteers to help with the testing. Once trained, the volunteers can save a lot of time with the skill checklists and routines assessments. You might use videotapes. Set up one or two video stations in the gymnasium and have children perform a skill or routine when it is ready or mastered. You can develop a bank of tapes over time to show development of skills or the growing complexity of routines at different grade levels. Although it is too time-consuming to grade every child by watching performances on a videotape, using videotapes is valid as a screen for the program's overall value and as a check to see whether children are improving over grade levels.

Psychomotor Assessment

Improvement in motor skills is a goal of many children's physical education programs. Testing for motor skills is far less common, however, than testing for physical fitness (Graham, 1992). The reason is that teachers believe many skill tests require a rather elaborate set-up and are difficult to administer quickly to classes. Using these suggestions will shorten the time it takes to test for motor skills substantially.

The I-Can Checklist

Teachers can make checklists similar to the one for rolling skills to assess traveling actions,

Directions:

When you judge your partner's sequence, use the coding system at the bottom of the page.

Name	Balance—stillness (3 counts)	Balance—base of support (1, 2, 3, 4)	Balance—level (high/medium/low)	Balance—inverted/upright	Balance—shape (stretch/curl/twist)	Balance—symmetrical/asymmetrical	Roll—type	Roll—direction	Transitions—smooth	Contrasts—time (fast/slow)
1. *Lauren A.*	Y	3,2	L,M	I,U	S,T	A,S	B	B	Y	S
2. *Amy L.*	Y	1,4	L,L	U,U	S,S	S,A	P	S	Y	F
3.										
4.										
5.										

Key

Balance—hold for 3 seconds	Y = yes; N = no.
Balance—base of support	Number of body parts supporting weight = 1, 2, 3, 4.
Balance—level	H = high; M = medium; L = low.
Balance—type	I = inverted; U = upright.
Balance—shape	S = stretch; C = curl; T = twist.
Balance—type	S = symmetrical; A = asymmetrical.
Roll—type	F = forward; B = backward; S = seated; P = pencil; E = egg.
Roll—direction	F = forward; B = backward; S = sideways.
Transition—smooth	Y = yes; N = no.
Contrasts—time	F = fast; S = slow.

Figure 5.2 Sample checklist for floor sequence.

balancing skills, tumbling skills, and other rotation skills (see Figure 5.1). Checklists can be on individual cards given to students or posted on the wall of a gym. When a child thinks she has mastered a given skill she can check it off, or have a partner or the teacher check the performance.

Assessing Critical Components

Motor skill testing often provides a quantitative score: how many, how far, how high. This is particularly true of the manipulative skills and games areas, where it is easy to keep score. In recent years there has been an increasing interest in assessing how children perform the qualitative components of a skill. This assessment is particularly suitable for gymnastics skills, in which process figures importantly.

The ultimate goal of qualitative assessment is to analyze whether a movement is mechanically correct. Often critical components, focal points, or developmental sequences of a given movement are analyzed for research purposes, using high-speed film or stop-action video. This is time-consuming and impractical for most teachers. It is more practical to develop checklists of critical components (see Figure 5.3) and use them as you give the children a task or movement sequence. Once the children start working, the teacher can step back and observe one critical component (cue, refinement) at a time. For example, you assign the children the task of doing a cartwheel on the floor or with a piece of equipment. While the children are practicing, you check to see if they are keeping their arms and legs straight; a general estimate can be obtained and recorded on a class list in 3 to 5 minutes.

The Physical Education Outcomes Committee of NASPE (Franck et al., 1991) developed a list of critical components or benchmarks in the areas of jumping, landing, rolling, balancing, and weight transfer which are helpful in assessing gymnastics skills. This information can help you in making your own checklists.

Some qualitative components are more easily observed for assessment than others. For example, it is easy to observe whether children can return to the feet at the end of a rolling action. It is more difficult to see whether the knees stay

tucked to the chest during the roll. Using stop-action videotapes occasionally can sharpen observation skills and obtain more reliable assessment. This method is not quick but it is worth doing occasionally to get a more accurate idea of what help the children need to refine skills.

Teachers from area schools can get together from time to time, perhaps once a month, to discuss the critical components of selected skills. You can compare checklists and discuss what is important to observe. Together watch a videotape of some children doing the skill under discussion, seeing if you are in agreement as to what you have or have not observed. This is another process that can sharpen observation skills.

Testing Routines and Sequences

While the development of specific individual skills is important in gymnastics, the ability to link the skills and create smooth transitions from one action or balance to another is even more important. At a beginning level, teachers might *test*

Directions:

Check all of the children for one critical component at a time. Use the coding system at the bottom of this chart for indicating your judgments.

Name	Arms and legs stretched	Hand, hand-foot, foot	Start/finish facing same direction	Smooth motion
1. *Devon B.*	Y	S	Y	Y
2. *Kevin H.*	Y	S	Y	Y
3. *Amy M.*	N	N	N	N
4. *Liz W.*	P	N	Y	N
5.				

Key

Arms and legs stretched	Y = yes, like spoke in wheel; P = partial, slightly bent; N = no, legs bent at knee by 90° or more
Hand, hand-foot, foot	S = sequential, one at a time in order; N = nonsequential, 2 hands, then 2 feet
Start/finish	Y = face same direction; N = one-quarter turn or twist
Smooth motion	Y = rhythmical (1, 2, 3, 4); N = nonrhythmical (quick or slow in hand and foot placement)

Figure 5.3 Sample checklist of critical components for cartwheels.

for inclusion. After calling for a sequence or routine at the end of a class period, a teacher quickly assesses whether the specified components are included. For example, when asking children to balance-travel-balance, the teacher scans to see if students have selected a balance that they can hold for 3 seconds, an appropriate traveling action, and a second balance that they again hold for 3 seconds to show control. Most children will show compliance with this type of task, and you will get a quick read on whether a child has understood your directions, a check for clarity.

A somewhat more complicated technique might be called *assessing for qualitative components and process variables*. Over time children should learn that variety, quality, contrast, and challenge are important parts of gymnastics sequences. Although assessing or judging gymnastics is subjective in nature, it is based on how well skills are executed and linked together. As a result, checklists such as the one in Figure 5.2 (see p. 39) can help make the children aware of the array of process variables possible in their sequence. Children should be encouraged and challenged to include variety and contrast as they create routines. If the first balance is at a low level on two body parts, a patch and a point, perhaps the second balance will be at a higher level on three body parts. If the first balance is upright, perhaps the second will be inverted. If one is symmetrical, the second would be asymmetrical. The rolling action could be slow and sustained or very sudden and quick, focusing on the time element during transition. Variety in definitive lines (extension out through the toes and fingers), angles at the joints, shape (stretch, curl, twist), and eye focus can further contrast and improve the quality in a routine.

Watching and evaluating each child's routine in each class is an impossible task. Student partners, high school or college students, or volunteer parents can assess a routine once at the end of a unit using a *qualitative component* or *process variable checklist*; this helps make qualitative assessment of children's sequence work manageable and realistic. Further, you can videotape and store from one year to the next the final routines of individuals or partners. This is authentic assessment and a nice way to show the development of skill and complexity of routines developed over the elementary school years.

Cognitive Assessment

There is a wealth of information that children should know about body management and applying mechanical principles to gymnastics. This has been well established by the NASPE Outcomes Project (Franck et al., 1991). Realistically, a teacher makes several decisions about what, when, and how to test the children's understanding of cognitive tests. First, test items should reflect what is taught in the gymnastics program, and second, testing needs to be manageable. Here are several ideas that are time-efficient and yet gather valuable information.

The Quick Written Test

When we think of assessing children's cognitive understanding, we usually think of some form of a standard paper and pencil test. To keep the procedure short, try developing a 5- to 10-question multiple choice (see Figure 5.4) or true-false (see Figure 5.5) test and administer it at

1. To run better you should:
   a. Swing your arms from side to side
   b. Stay up on the balls of your feet
   c. Bounce up and down
   d. Get a good backward lean

2. A skip could be described as a:
   a. Jump, hop
   b. Hop, jump
   c. Step, hop
   d. Hop, step

3. If you are trying to jump onto or over a bench, what should you do to help jump higher?
   a. Keep your legs straight before you jump.
   b. Stand on your toes before you jump.
   c. Bend your knees before you jump.
   d. I don't know.

4. Which of the following are forms of weight transfer?
   a. Feet only
   b. Hands and feet
   c. Adjacent body parts
   d. All of the above

5. Which of these is a pathway you could use while traveling on your feet?
   a. Curved
   b. Forward
   c. Direct
   d. Backward

Figure 5.4 Sample multiple choice questions about traveling actions.

1. To increase your balance or stability in a chosen statue-like shape, you could lower your center of gravity by bending.
   ❏ True   ❏ False

2. To increase your balance or stability in a chosen statue-like shape, you could make your base more narrow by pulling your supports closer together.
   ❏ True   ❏ False

3. You will remain balanced and still, even if your center of gravity shifts outside your base of support.
   ❏ True   ❏ False

4. In general, you will have better balance if you have three body parts touching the ground than if you have only one part while you are trying to stay still.
   ❏ True   ❏ False

5. You can only balance if you are in a symmetrical shape. If you are in an asymmetrical shape you cannot balance.
   ❏ True   ❏ False

Figure 5.5 Sample true-false questions about the principles of balance.

the beginning or end of a class. As an alternative, create a testing station in a quiet corner of the gym which each child can visit briefly during the class. Either way, the test should not take more than 10 minutes to administer, and it would give a quick assessment of a child's understanding of the given skill(s) or principle(s).

Another way to check for understanding quickly is to have the children write out the major cues necessary to perform a given skill (see Figure 5.6). A cue is a component critical for the successful execution of a skill. Before class set out paper and pencils for each child in an area away from gymnastics activities. Three by five (or 5 × 8) cards work well if you are outdoors. At some point in the lesson, ask the children to go to this area and respond to a cues question about a skill. As soon as the children are finished, they can resume activity. This cognitive assessment takes less than 5 minutes of class time.

The most effective questions are those you design to assess what is being taught in the program (Graham, 1992). Good questions take time to write. Often you will want to revise questions,

based on the children's responses and levels of understanding. In time, however, you can develop a battery of questions that indicate what children are learning in gymnastics. By asking only a few questions at a time, you will not feel overburdened with scoring and record-keeping. For example, by asking 5 to 10 questions three times a semester, testing and grading can be accomplished in manageable blocks of time. Different classes or grades can be tested at different times in the term. Rather than correct several hundred tests of thirty questions in a single weekend, limit testing to a quick check for understanding during the unit of instruction.

Checking for Understanding

It is also possible to assess how well children understand a concept in a quick test. To check for understanding (Graham, 1992) simply ask the children to demonstrate comprehension of a particular skill, concept, or process variable by stating the cues, focal points, or critical components. Besides verbalizing understanding, students can also demonstrate the skill. For example, you might give the children these kinds of instructions.

- "Tell me the cues for doing the cartwheel properly."
- "Show me where and how to place your hands on the floor when you do a backward roll."
- "Tell me the proper cues for taking weight on your hands to transfer it into a handstand."
- "Show me three ways to resolve a forward roll or to come out of a shoulder stand."

A scan will quickly let you know how well the children have understood the skill or concept. Of course, simply knowing how to do it doesn't mean they will always perform the skill correctly, but it is a necessary first step. This check for understanding is an excellent *closure* to a lesson; the class reviews the one or two cues, or *reminder words*, (see chapters 6 to 8), that you have emphasized during the learning experience.

Poker Chip Survey

Another way to survey the children to determine how well they have understood a cognitive concept is to have them place poker chips, straws, popsicle sticks, or other such items in a container. At the end of a class you demonstrate a roll

Your friend, Trapezoid, doesn't know how to do a forward roll very well. List five things that would help her become better at doing the forward roll.

1. Hands on floor, thumbs pointed in
2. Bottom up in air
3. Look between legs
4. Stay in a ball
5. Return to feet

Figure 5.6   You can check for children's understanding with open-ended questions.

incorrectly, for example, using the hands on the floor to help push up in returning to the feet. Ask the children, as they leave the class, to put a red chip, straw, or stick in the box if the roll was done correctly, and a blue chip, straw, or stick if the roll was done incorrectly. A quick survey of the colors placed in the container will tell you how well the children have understood the concept.

Affective Assessment

There are also several methods teachers can use to assess the attitudes and values of the class toward gymnastics. Children's attitudes and values can be important barometers indicating their likelihood of developing active, healthy lifestyles in adulthood.

Smiley-Face Exit Poll

A simple way to learn how children feel is to survey them in a manner similar to the poker chip survey. This time, however, laminate a number of cartoon faces: smiley, neutral, and frowny (Graham, 1992). As children leave the gym, they are asked to pick the face that best represents their feelings about their ability or enjoyment of the lesson from one of the three boxes (smiley, neutral, frowny) by the door and deposit it in the ballot box. These are some sample questions and statements to give them.

- How do you feel about your ability to do rolls?
- How do you feel about your ability to balance?
- Gymnastics makes me feel stronger.
- Gymnastics makes me feel more flexible.
- How do you feel about designing your own sequence in the next gymnastics class?
- How do you feel about today's lesson?

Paper-and-Pencil Surveys

As with questions assessing cognitive understanding, attitude questions can effectively be part of a paper-and-pencil survey and reveal a lot of information. The sample questions in

Figure 5.7 suggest ways that a teacher might assess the children's feelings and attitudes.

Aesthetic Valuing

In 1990 the South Carolina Department of Education adopted a curricular framework for dance education that included four components that are relevant also to gymnastics. The first component is *aesthetic perception*, which includes what the body can do in gymnastics (psychomotor domain). The second and third components are the *creative process* and *cultural heritage*, inclusive of what we know about gymnastics (cognitive domain). The fourth component is *aesthetic valuing*, or what a child learns to appreciate and value in gymnastics (affective domain). Little attention has been given the area of aesthetics. Still, the implications of what might be done to work on values will broaden our concepts of literacy and what it means to be a physically educated person. Just as people judge and appreciate a piece of art, music, or literature, so too should children learn to apply aesthetic principles and choreographic criteria in viewing gymnastic sequences, whether as an observer or as a participant.

Without getting too complicated or sophisticated, give children opportunities to exercise their abilities to appreciate, judge, and value gymnastics. Here are a few suggestions.

- "Watch your partner's sequence and tell them one thing you really like about the performance."
- "See if your partner uses good mechanical principles for balance. Tell them what they are doing well. What could they improve upon?"
- "Watch the shapes your partner creates with their body during their sequences. Are they symmetrical or asymmetrical? Upright or inverted? Did you notice any changes in level and the base of support? Tell your partner which shapes really caught your eye."
- "Watch the transitions in your partner's sequence. Are they smooth? Are there any stops, breaks, extra steps, or extra movements? Compliment your partner when you see the movement flow from one move to the next."
- "Watch your partner's sequence. Suggest one way they could change a balance, roll, or locomotor action to make the sequence better or more challenging."
- (For older elementary school students) "You are a gymnastics judge at the Olympics. You can award 10 points for routines—2 points for locomotor actions, 2 points for rotation, 2 points for balance, 2 points for smooth transition, and 2 points for overall aesthetic appeal. This includes the variety of changes in level, direction, pathway, time, and force in the routines. Get in groups of four, watch and judge each other's routines, and award points. You may deduct .25 or .50 for any errors you see in any category."

1. I like to roll, tumble, and do cartwheels at home and out on the playground.

   ☐ Yes   ☐ No

2. I like doing balance activities with a partner.

   ☐ Yes   ☐ No

3. I like making up sequences in gymnastics.

   ☐ Yes   ☐ No

4. If gymnastics is on television, I would watch it.

   ☐ Yes   ☐ No

5. I would like to get extra gymnastics lessons outside of school.

   ☐ Yes   ☐ No

6. How do you feel about your ability to jump onto and off of boxes or benches?

7. How do you feel about your ability to roll on the floor or a mat?

8. How do you feel about your ability to balance upside down?

9. How do you feel about your ability to balance on a piece of equipment?

10. How do you feel about your ability to vault over objects?

Figure 5.7 Sample questions designed to evaluate children's feelings and attitudes toward gymnastics.

Logs, journals, and discussion circles also provide valuable insights about how and what children are learning as well as clues about developing value systems (see Graham, 1992, chapter 12 for more information on using these techniques).

Grading

I agree with Graham (1992) about the inadequacies of grading in elementary physical education. Providing a letter grade or even an S/U for 400 to 600 children at least two times each year is a challenging task, and the grade actually provides parents very little information about their child's progress in physical education. Developing a physical education progress report, sent home as an insert with the child's regular report card one or more times per year, is perhaps a better system (see the appendix).

In gymnastics this progress report could include a checklist of the skills learned during the year. A qualitative checklist would show uses of or focal points mastered on selected skills; as an alternative it might record graded performances on sequences or routines at the end of a unit on gymnastics. This kind of a progress report informs parents much more about what their children are learning in physical education.

Summary

There are numerous examples of ways to assess children in the psychomotor, cognitive, and affective domains in this chapter, and some will be more attractive than others to different teachers. Some assessment methods invite frequent use, and others may never be used. As teachers we select assessment tools that work for us, given the time and class sizes in a program. We need to be smart about assessment.

A well thought-out assessment program has two advantages. First, it indicates to us the progress the children are making in developing skills, knowledge, and values. Second, assessment allows us to share some relatively objective information about what children are learning in physical education with parents, school boards, and administrators. In this era of accountability, an assessment program provides an important way to demonstrate the program's value for children.

Part II

Teaching Developmentally Appropriate Learning Experiences in Gymnastics

The second part of the book includes three chapters that describe in detail how gymnastics might be developed for teaching children. Each chapter consists of a number of learning experiences (LEs) from which lessons can be developed. From each LE, for example, you might be able to develop two or more lessons, depending on your teaching situation. It is important to realize, however, that in many instances if one were to teach an entire LE as a lesson, the children would no doubt finish confused—and probably frustrated—because LEs contain far more than can be reasonably taught, and learned, in one 30-minute experience. Most LEs contain several objectives. For most lessons you will want to select one, maybe two, objectives to concentrate on. In other words, you want to pick a "learnable piece" that children can truly understand and grasp—rather than simply exposing them to ideas that can't be understood, let alone learned, in the time allotted.

The learning experiences in Part II are organized according to a similar format. This format is as follows:

- The *Name* of the learning experience
- *Objectives* that explain the psychomotor, cognitive, and affective skills children will improve as a result of participating in this learning experience. When appropriate, the NASPE benchmarks that these objectives are helping students meet are referenced at the end of an objective in parentheses. The first character refers to the grade level the benchmark is found under in the official NASPE document, and the second gives the number of the benchmark itself.
- A *Suggested Grade Range* for the learning experience
- The *Organization* that children will be working in during the learning experience
- The kinds and amounts of *Equipment Needed* for presenting this learning experience to children
- A *Description* of the total learning experience, explained as if the physical education teacher was actually presenting the learning experience to children (additional information for teachers is set off in brackets)
- *Look For*, which gives key points for teachers to keep in mind when informally observing children's progress in the learning experience. These are related to the objectives for the LE.
- *How Can I Change This?*, which allows you to either increase or decrease the difficulty

level involved in the learning experience, thus allowing for all students to be challenged at their ability levels

- *Teachable Moments*, those perfect opportunities either during or after a lesson to discuss how a cognitive or affective concept is related to what has occurred in the learning experience

Each of these chapters is organized around one skill theme in educational gymnastics (see Figure 3.1): traveling, statics, or rotation. Within each chapter work is further divided into categories. Categories of traveling in chapter 6 include steplike actions using the feet; steplike actions using the hands, feet, and knees; weight transfer; and flight. Characteristics, principles, and types of balance are the categories of statics in chapter 7. Chapter 8 focuses on the principles of rotation, movement around three axes, and rotation of the body. The process variables of human movement—body, space, effort, and relationships (see Table 3.4)—support all work.

Learning experiences do not develop in only one dimension. Although one skill theme is chosen as the primary focus in each LE, other skill themes are used to support the development of that concept through sequence work. The themes develop parallel to and dependent on one another. What this means is that a lesson will never be only about forward rolls, cartwheels, balances, or jumping and landing. Rather, after a warm-up period, the main focus of the lesson is developed. New material is learned and refined. Then, a sequence is developed that integrates the main focus with other previously learned skills. For example, if the children work on rolling skills, by the end of the lesson they might integrate a jump, hop, land, and roll of choice, finishing in a balance at a low level.

The concept behind the lessons is to focus on specific skill development and then to combine that skill with others in logical pieces of work. For example, students learning to perform rolls may link two different rolls together with a balance. Students focusing on traveling actions may jump, jump, jump with a turn or shape, land, and resolve the movement with a balance.

Important to the idea of linking actions is the concept of a sequence. All gymnastics work should have a beginning, middle, and end. The beginning may be a held position of readiness or a balance pose which is a signal that the gymnast is about to begin. The middle consists of the action phase in which all work is linked together aesthetically, with an emphasis on good lines, smooth flow from one action to another, and a focus on the important aspects of the work. The ending position is a clear stop, or signal that the work is completed.

Each of the next three chapters consists of eight learning experiences. Although each chapter focuses on one of the principal categories of the content, feel free to subdivide the LEs into more than one class. Use the ideas for changing an experience or emphasize the teachable moment information. Each learning experience may stand by itself or carry over into several sessions, perhaps comprising a mini-unit of instruction.

Chapter 6

Learning Experiences for Traveling

This chapter includes eight learning experiences (LEs) within the skill theme of traveling. LEs have been developed for the four categories of traveling, which include steplike actions using the feet; steplike actions using the hands, feet, and knees; weight transfer; and flight. The following outline provides a quick glance at the focus and suggested grade range for each learning experience.

Focus	Name	Suggested grade range
Steplike actions using feet: walk, run, hop, jump	And Away We Go	Pre-K–1
Steplike actions using hands, feet, knees: feet to hands to feet	Bunny-Hop	1–2
Flight: hurdle or spring takeoffs	Ready for Takeoff	1–2
Weight transfer: rocking, rolling, sliding	Break Dance in Slow Motion	2–3
Flight: shapes in air, vaulting	Fantasy Flight	2–3
Steplike actions using hands, feet, knees: feet to hands to feet	Clockface	4–6
Weight transfer: under equipment	Beam Me Up	5–6
Variety of traveling actions: relationships to a partner	Me and My Shadow	5–6

AND AWAY WE GO

Objectives

As a result of participating in this learning experience, children will improve their ability to

- use their feet to travel by exploring each of the five basic steplike actions (1-2, #4)
- combine steplike actions while changing directions, pathways, and speeds, with smooth transitions between actions
- describe fundamental differences between walking, running, hopping, and jumping

Suggested Grade Range

Primary (Pre-K–1)

Organization

A large open space is needed. Children spread out in personal space.

Equipment Needed

A variety of pieces of small equipment is helpful—hoops, ropes, paper or wooden wands supported by 2 milk crates. One piece of equipment for each child is appropriate.

Description

"As we begin I would like everyone sitting like a gymnast [long sit–pike position]. Right—legs together, back straight, head up, toes pointed. This is our "gymnast-sit." See if you can bend over and reach for your toes when you're sitting like a gymnast. Let your knees bend a little bit. This time keep your head down close to your knees and let's count together to 10. Good! Now sit up and rock back onto your shoulders with your legs up in the air [support hips with hands, elbows bent on floor]. This is called a shoulder stand. Straddle your legs wide apart side by side, just like a big "V." Scissors your legs with one forward and one back. Change back to a V-straddle. Let's hold each position and count out loud to ten. Do you feel the muscles in your legs and back stretch? Sit back up, straddle your legs apart on the floor in front of you. Now lean forward; see if you can move your chest and head close to the floor in front of you. OK, back to your "gymnast-sit"—legs together in front. Put your hands by your hips and rise up into a back support position [tight body], just like I'm doing. Good! See if you can turn over into a front support position [push-up position]. Now, let your tummy sag down to the floor, then arch up like an angry cat. Try that again—sagging tummy, angry cat. Good stretching! Now, let's put all of this together. See if you can follow what I say. Ready? [Say each cue as students perform.] Gymnast-sit—touch your toes—rock back to a shoulder stand—gymnast sit—rise into a back support—turn over to front support—turn again to a back support—now go into a gymnast-sit. Did you feel your muscles stretch way out?

"See all of the equipment out on the floor? When I say so, I'd like all the girls to nicely get one piece, take it to your personal space, and sit down beside it. Go. Boys . . . Go. You did that very safely! This time, when I say go, we will begin running *softly* in, out, and around all of the equipment in general space. Visit all of the places in the gym, and be careful not to bump into other children or other equipment. This is not a race. I'll be looking for high knees and light, springy feet like this [demonstrate]. Go. Good, I like how you're picking your knees up and moving with light feet! Run a little faster [move feet quickly]. Now slower. I see a few people change pathways so they don't run into other people. That's good! Now take long running steps. OK, now short quick steps. Can you run forward? . . . backward? . . . sideways? How about running straight [curved, zigzag]? Let's use walking steps this time and do the same things. Walk fast—now slow. Long steps! Short steps. Forward [backward, sideways, straight, curved, zigzag]. Good! Stop where you are.

"Walking and running involve transfer of weight from one foot to the other. What is it called when we step from one foot to the same foot? [Demonstrate.] That's right, Allan, it is a hop. Let's do what we just did, only this time, I'm looking for great hops. Don't forget to use both right and left feet. Go. Fast hops—slow hops. Let's see long hops. [Vary with short hops, hops forward, backward, sideways; in straight, curved zigzag pathways.] Use your arms to help you hop! Stop; let's take a rest.

"Next we will try jumping. Do you know there are three ways we can use our feet when we jump? We can jump from one foot to two [demonstrate], two feet to two feet [demonstrate], and two feet to one foot [demonstrate]. Try to see if you can do these in your own space. Try one foot to two [two to two, two to one; let them try each jump a few times]. Use all three of these when you travel this time. Go! [Call out the different ways; vary speeds, length of jumps, directions and pathways.]

"Remember, bend and explode to get super jumps! Use light and springy feet like a bunny. Land softly on the front [balls] of your feet. Bend your knees when you land to make it soft. Stop.

"Now let's experiment with our feet as we travel about the space. Pick one of the steplike actions we've done. That means you can walk, hop, or jump. Watch me first. I'll pick jumping from two feet to two feet [demonstrate]. Now I'll jump up to and over a piece of equipment. See how I keep using this jump to go to the next piece of equipment? Now watch—I can hop *close to*, then *into*, and even *over* a hoop. Then I hop to the next piece of equipment. When I say "go," you pick your favorite way to move. Make sure you go to all the open spaces and go to lots of equipment. Go! [Signal stop.]

"Go back home to your first piece of equipment. Do you remember where it was? It's OK if you don't—just find one! For our final task we are going to make a *sequence*. That means we will put the actions together. You will work only in your personal space and with your piece of equipment. Start a couple steps away from your equipment. See if you can use three different steplike actions—the hops, jumps, and walk—to move *toward*, *over*, and *away* from your equipment. Watch me. Instead of using all hops this time, I'm going to try *different* steps. I can hop toward the equipment, use one or two feet over the rope, and jump with both feet away from the rope. I used three different actions. Now you try it. I'm going to see if you can use three different actions, too. Good! Try it again, another way! [Signal stop.] Now show me the one way you like best. Do it three times. Very good. I can see that you are really working hard and using your feet to travel in different ways. You are going into, out of, over, and around your piece of equipment [signal stop].

"Who can tell me what you do with your feet when you walk and run? That's right; one foot to the other is walking and running. Hop? Yes, one foot to the same is hopping. Jump? Yes—there are three different jumps—two feet to two feet, two feet to one foot, and one foot to two feet. That is all for today. Show me one of the steplike actions as you safely line up to go back to your classroom."

Look For

- This is not a race. Emphasis should be on quality locomotor patterns. Soft feet, high knees, use of the arms to assist traveling actions, and erect posture, or body carriage (see Figure 6.1), are all important. Choose one or two of these to emphasize.

- Focus on smooth transitions from one action to another. Encourage the children to move smoothly from a hop to a jump or to a step without stopping or taking extra stutter steps.

Figure 6.1   Children should use a variety of high-quality, steplike actions to travel about the equipment.

How Can I Change This?

- Introduce concepts of speed, direction, relationship of body parts, or pathways in the sequence work. For example, do long, powerful two feet jumps with the feet wide apart on the approach; jump using two feet with a half turn in the air over equipment to a landing on one foot; or take quick steps away from a hurdle while running zigzag forward or backward.

- Add a roll and/or a balance to the sequence. For example, hop toward the equipment, jump over it, land, roll, and finish in a balance.

> ### TEACHABLE MOMENTS
>
> Children can develop word cues for their sequences: for example, step-step-hop-turn-jump-jump-jump.
>
> Some children may be able to choreograph and notate the sequences (see the appendix): for example, J2 to 1, J1 to 2, 3 × F; J2 to 1, 1/4 T; 1H, 4 × S to denote jump two feet to one, then one foot to two feet three times forward; jump two feet to one with a quarter-turn over the hurdle; one foot hop four times sideways.

BUNNY-HOP

Objectives

As a result of participating in this learning experience, children will improve their ability to

- use steplike weight transfer actions of the hands, knees, and feet in a variety of conditions both on the floor and on equipment (1-2, #8)
- use steplike weight transfer actions of the hands, knees, and feet as a primary means to link with other traveling and balancing actions
- understand that steplike weight transfer actions of the hands, knees, and feet are a type of traveling action

Suggested Grade Range

Primary (1–2)

Organization

A large open space is needed. A variety of small equipment—such as hula hoops, wands, and ropes; and large equipment such as benches and boxes—should be spread out with adequate distance between pieces for safety.

Equipment Needed

A piece of small equipment such as a hula hoop, wand, or rope is needed for each child. A box or bench is needed for every 2 children. Mats or carpet squares are needed for padding beside the boxes and benches.

Description

"See all of the equipment out on the floor? We'll start today by staying *away* from it. When we travel around the equipment, let's not touch any of it. Let's start with running. Remember, high knees, light feet. Go! [Signal stop.] Use a straight pathway now [then zigzag and curved pathways]. Let's change directions. Try forward. OK. Now go sideways. Good! When I say go, run backward. First move to open spaces, away from others. Go! [Signal stop.] Now let's skip. I want good skips, with high knees and swinging arms. [Signal stop.] Let's change pathways and directions [call out]. Now slide—go sideways one way. [Stop.] Now move in the other direction. Use light feet; glide across the floor.

"Stop. Sit down in a personal space. We have been using our feet to travel all around the room. There are other ways we can move, too. Today we are going to use our hands *and* feet to help us go somewhere. Let's see how many ways there are. Put your tummy facing the floor. Who can travel about the floor using two hands and one foot? Good! How about using two feet and one hand? Try two feet and two hands. Travel slowly, this is not a race! [Try these, changing directions—forward, backward, sideways—and pathways—straight, curved, and zigzag.] What about hands and knees? I see two hands, two knees. Two hands, one knee. Two knees, one hand. Change directions, pathways. Excellent.

"Next, put your tummy up, facing the ceiling. Now show me different ways you can walk on your hands and feet. I see two hands and one foot . . . two feet and one hand . . . two hands and two feet. Take a rest! There sure are a lot of ways to move using our hands, knees, and feet.

"Find a small piece of equipment to sit beside—a hoop, a wand, or a rope. Go! We are going to experiment with different ways we can move into, out of, over, and around our piece of equipment using our hands and feet. First, let's *alternate*, or change from hand to foot. Hand, foot, hand, foot [demonstrate]. That's like walking. Use the alternating pattern to move into, out of, over, or around your equipment several times. Stop and rest. Next, we'll try *twos*. Move your hand and foot on one side, then on the other side [demonstrate alternating sides] to travel about your piece of equipment. Stop.

"Now let's try twos a different way. We will use two hands and two feet [belly down; demonstrate]. We call that a *bunny-hop*. That's it. Two hands, then two feet. Use the bunny-hop to move into, out of, over, and around your equipment. You can go forward and backward. Good! Now twist your body and put the hands down, feet to the right; now hands down, feet to the left. OK, stop and sit down.

"We're going to start using the large equipment next—the boxes and benches. I want you to use a steplike action to travel on your feet. You can hop, jump, or skip on the floor. [Demonstrate and talk children through.] When you get to a box or bench, then use your hands and feet to travel onto, off of, along, from side to side around your equipment. Then jump, hop, or skip to another box or bench. Got it? OK, go. [As they practice, give cues.] Use your hands and feet in different ways. Remember, you can use two hands and one foot, alternate, use twos, or bunny-hops. Stop. Did you find that some of these ways work better than others? For now, let's just do bunny-hops on the boxes and benches. Put both hands on the box or bench. Keep your fingers spread and the arms straight. That's important. Your shoulders are over your hands. Kick up with two feet. Come down softly onto the bench or box on your two feet. Take turns, or alternate, using your hands and feet. Travel over the box or bench, along it, and side-to-side.

"To end this class, we'll make up a sequence. We will link together different actions. First, *travel* on the floor using only your feet. You can hop, jump, or skip. You can change directions and pathways as you move. When you get to a box or bench, do bunny-hops over and along it, side-to-side. Move to the floor and safely lower your body to a mat or carpet square and do a *roll* of your choice, then return to your feet. Do all of that again. So, you travel, bunny-hop, roll, then begin all over again. Any questions? Go.

"Stop. Everyone come in. Who can tell me some of the ways we used our hands, knees, and feet to move or transfer our weight as we traveled around the room today? That's right, Tomiko, two hands and a foot. Yes, Matt, two hands and two feet. There are sure a lot of ways we can use our body parts to travel along the floor and on equipment. You are getting very good at traveling while using different steplike actions. That's it for now. See you soon."

Look For

- Strong use of the arms; the arms must be straight.
- Weight on hands and/or feet (Figure 6.2). No flopping or crashing.
- Children keeping a tight tummy and bottom: no sagging.
- Good transition or linking actions in movement from floor to equipment. Keep momentum going. One action leads into the next.

How Can I Change This?

- Include small equipment in the sequence. Travel on the hands and feet in, out, over, or along the small equipment to arrive at the large equipment. Travel on hands and feet over, along, around, onto, and off of the box or bench. Roll. Move on to another piece of equipment and continue.
- Add a balance (e.g., travel, bunny-hop, roll, balance).
- Stay in one place. Place a piece of small equipment near a box or bench. Develop a repeatable sequence using feet-hand-feet weight transfer in one station, rather than traveling around the gym.

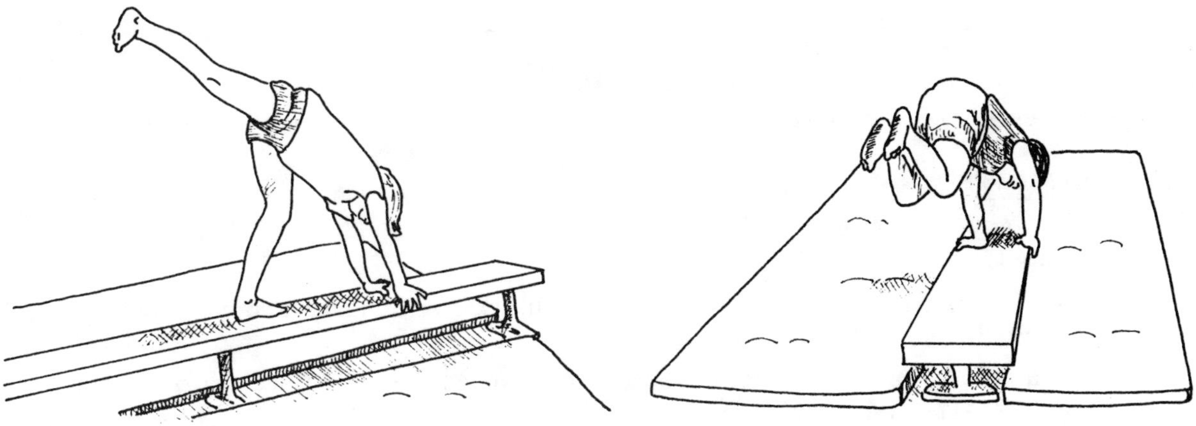

Figure 6.2   Children should use their hands and feet to travel on the large equipment.

TEACHABLE MOMENTS

Question the children about traveling. What is traveling? What body parts can they use to travel? How is using both hands and feet similar to using only the feet? (Steplike) How is using both the hands and feet similar to weight transfer? (Hands and feet when placed next to each other are adjacent.) Weight transfer and steplike actions form a category, type, or set of actions that helps our bodies travel from one place to another.

Have children observe how insects and animals move. Inchworms, caterpillars, snails, spiders, snakes, bears, horses, and monkeys use their bodies in different ways. Compare these with possible human movements.

READY FOR TAKEOFF

Objectives

As a result of participating in this learning experience, children will improve their ability to

- develop a 1- to 2-foot takeoff as a powerful, explosive means to propel the body into the air (1-2, #4)
- attempt a variety of stretched, curled, and twisted shapes in the air during flight (1-2, #17)
- understand the necessity of powerful, thrusting actions of the arms and legs in a vertical direction to gain lift

Suggested Grade Range

Primary (1–2)

Organization

A large open space is needed. Children spread out with one or two to a box, bench, or trampette.

Equipment Needed

Use available mats. Children need a place to jump from: A 12" to 15" box, milk crate, bench, stacked newspapers in a cardboard box, or a trampette all would be acceptable. Hula hoops or a rope are useful.

Description

"Today we are going to be jumping up high into the air. While we are in the air, we will make shapes. Let's begin now by jogging about on the floor—not too fast. Lift your knees high, and jog with a light spring up on the balls of your feet. Jog to open spaces. Be careful not to bump! Stop! Watch me quickly! This time, as you run toward someone, eyeball them. Look at them like this [demonstrate]. As you get close to them, change directions, and fade slowly away [fade]. Move quickly toward someone, but fade slowly away. Think of the speeds you're using. Go. [Let them repeat several times.] Stop!

Now we are going to work on a specific type of jumping. It's called a *hurdle jump* or *spring takeoff*, and looks like this [demonstrate]. Have you ever seen people do this? What were they doing? Yes, Jenna, divers and gymnasts jump this way to *vault* and get *high* into the air. As you can see, there are hula hoops in different places on the floor. I'd like you to jog toward a hoop, like this [demonstrate]. Take one last step outside the hoop and land on two feet in the hoop. Land softly and bend down in a crouch. Then, move on and repeat this jump several times. Practice this. Go. Good, you're landing nice and softly, balanced on two feet. Stop. Now, this time, from your crouch, I want you to use your arms and legs to explode high into the air, and still land with both feet in the hoop. So, you'll jog, land, crouch, explode, and land again. Try that; go! [As the children practice, talk them through the sequence.] Push hard with your legs. Swing your arms up high. Look toward the ceiling and reach for the sky! [Repeat several times.] I'm looking for good jumps and soft, balanced landings on two feet. [Signal stop.]

"Let's go back to running toward people. As you approach someone, use your hurdle jump and give your friend high fives. Push with your legs hard and swing your arms up to get high. Land, then move on to another friend. Any questions? Go! [Students run, approach, high-five, land, move away. Stop.]

"Think now about what you can do with your body while it is in the air. What shapes can it make? wide? narrow? stretched? bent? twisted? symmetrical or asymmetrical? What are your arms and legs doing while you are in the air? [Show pictures as examples.] Using the hula hoops again, you'll run, approach, hurdle, jump, make a shape, and land. Who would like to demonstrate this for us? OK, Rina. Notice how she runs, approaches the hoop, hurdles and jumps into it, makes a shape, lands, and then moves on. Let's see you practice this. Go! [During practice give cues.] Try several shapes. Make your shape when you're high up in the air. Bend your knees quickly to land under control. Stop.

"Next, we will take our jumping to the equipment. Remember to use your arms and legs to help you explode up and out high. You'll jog, approach the equipment, hurdle onto it, jump (or make a rebound) off, make a shape, and land. [Demonstrate or have a student demonstrate.] Jump onto and off of the bench in one fluid movement—that's called a rebound. Use the momentum from landing on the bench to carry you high into the air as you rebound and jump off the bench. Reach for the sky. Go! [As children practice, give them reminders.] See if you can do the same shapes in the air, jumping off the bench as you did when you jumped from the floor. Keep moving, or traveling, around the floor and visit each bench or box as you try making several different shapes in the air. [Signal stop.]

"For the last activity today, I want you to stay at one box or bench. Do the same sequence [jog, approach, jump on, rebound off, shape, land]. This time, however, I want you to choose one shape for when you are in the air. It may be your best or your favorite shape. Practice it several times. Show your sequence to a partner near you. Go! [Signal stop.]

"Come in quickly. Who can tell me the name of the jump we were working on today? Yes, Latasha, a hurdle jump. What body parts help us get high in the air? Yes, Zachary, the *arms* reach for the sky, and the *legs* to crouch and explode. What kinds of shapes did you make during flight? Yes, Ryan, a stretch, curl, twist. Very good. See you next time."

Look For

- Good timing. Children will tend to start the shape too early while still on the floor. It is essential to get a good jump first. The key is the explosive power in the legs and a powerful arm thrust up (crouch—explode—reach). The shape should occur at the peak of suspension, and be done quickly: in and out of the shape, prepare to land.
- Proper landing. Children must recover from their shapes in the air quickly to land on the feet. Control is important: no crashing allowed.
- Variety. Children should try different shapes: stretched, bent, twisted, wide, narrow, symmetrical, and asymmetrical (see Figure 6.3).

How Can I Change This?

- Have the children create a similar sequence on the floor using a hula hoop or rope, but add a weight transfer action and a balance. An example might be to jog, approach, jump, shape in the air, land on the feet in a hoop, use a weight transfer action out of the hoop (cartwheel, roll, rock), and finish in a balance. Children should stay at their own hoops or ropes. Have them repeat the sequence several times and then choose their best work and show it to a partner.
- Have the children repeat the same sequence at their box, bench, or trampette, but add a balance at the end: jog, approach, jump, rebound, shape in air, land, resolve, and balance. *Resolve* means to make a smooth transition of your choice from landing on two feet into a balance position. Balances may be on the feet or the weight transferred into balanced positions on other body parts.

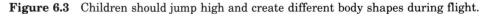

Figure 6.3   Children should jump high and create different body shapes during flight.

TEACHABLE MOMENTS

Bring pictures of athletes, dancers, and gymnasts into class to illustrate the use of body shapes during flight. Point out the relationships and transfer from one sport to another.

Relate shapes in the air to different balance positions (e.g., pike, straddle, squat).

BREAK DANCE IN SLOW MOTION

Objectives

As a result of participating in this learning experience, children will improve their ability to

- use rocking, rolling, and sliding actions as a means to travel from one body position to another
- understand that a traveling action, including weight transfer, can move the body a very short distance, as well as a long distance, across the floor
- use weight transfer actions to approach, mount, travel on, and/or dismount a piece of equipment (3-4, #26)

Suggested Grade Range

Primary (2–3)

Organization

A large open space is needed with mats, benches, and boxes spread out at a safe distance from each other. Mats should be placed beside each bench or box.

Equipment Needed

1 mat and bench or box for each student is needed for this activity.

Description

"Let's start today with everyone on a mat or the floor in a gymnast-sit, or long sitting position. Bend over and reach for your toes. Hold and count to 10 or 15. OK. Sit back up and place your hands on the floor. Press up into a back-support position with your tummy and bottom tight. You should have a good, long straight body. See if you can lift one arm up and turn your body into a push-up [front-support] position. Good! Let's start with the back-support position and do this all again, only this time you'll slide your feet toward your hands in the front-support position, lean forward, and place your forehead on the floor [demonstrate: tripod position]. Then you can place your knees on your elbows, and if you want to try it, you can then slowly raise your legs into a headstand [demonstrate]. Practice this a few times. [Signal start and stop]. This time, when your legs are back down, tuck your chin to your chest and go into a forward roll; finish in a long sitting position. It's important to tuck in your chin. We'll do the whole thing five times: sit and reach; now back-support position. Turn to a front support. Now slide down with your forehead on the floor in a tripod. Press up into a headstand, and down. Tuck, and roll. Any questions? [Repeat several times.]

"OK. Everyone up. Let's see some good jogging between the mats, with your knees high, soft landings, and when you get to a mat, make a nice high jump. Make a shape in the air, land, and do a roll of your choice; then return to your feet. Keep doing this—run, jump, shape, land, roll. Make different shapes each time in the air and use different rolls. [Signal stop.]

"Now, we'll add the benches or boxes. Who would like to demonstrate? OK, Brian and Marta. Start with good running on the floor. Jump onto the equipment. Jump off high, making a shape in the air. Swing your arms up. Land softly—squish! Roll on the mat, return to your feet, and continue. Good, you two! Everyone, try to visit each piece of equipment, and travel to open spaces, so you don't have to wait. [Signal start and stop.]

"Everyone, sit beside a mat near a piece of equipment. Remember the sequence when we first warmed up today? Gymnast-sit, back support, front support, tripod, press, tuck, and roll? Yes? Good thinking. When you did that sequence, did your body end up in the same place on the mat or floor as when you started the sequence? No. It moved just a little distance away, didn't it? When we move from one body part to another we call that *weight transfer*. Weight transfer occurs when we do a rock, roll, or slide action. Let's look for it.

"Everyone kneel on your hands and knees. Get your hips over your knees. Begin to let yourself down, moving to one side or the other, to the right or left. Feel your weight on your thigh, then the hip, then side, and into a shoulder stand. (See Traveling, And Away We Go, and Statics, Shoulder Stand for a complete description of a shoulder stand.) Round your body. Make the weight transfer smooth. Watch me [demonstrate]. Use this nice, rocking action to transfer your weight from a kneeling balance to a shoulder-stand balance. Practice this a few times.

"From your shoulder stand, go right into a backward shoulder roll to a knee and a foot balance. [Demonstrate and give children time to practice it.] Can you do it without putting your hands down on the floor in the beginning? Make your body round. You want smooth weight transfers. OK. Stop.

"Let's try a long pencil position on your tummy. Pull your body forward, sliding it into a push-up or front-support position. *Sliding* is also a way to transfer weight. Try this a couple times. Pull your body forward! Good [signal stop]. I want you to experiment now. Choose one body position and think of how you could use a slide, rock, or roll to help you travel from it smoothly into a new body position. Use different body parts and surfaces, and transfer your weight in different directions. Practice as many different ways as you can. Good, I see Li in a seated straddle with a turn over onto one thigh into a straddle push-up position. Sonny's doing a shoulder stand to a rock into two knees. Keep it up. Try several new ways!

"OK. Finally, we can use these weight transfer actions to help us travel to and get on or off equipment. For example, we can use a roll to arrive at a box or bench. If we are really tricky, we can even use a roll to *mount* or get up on the box or bench. The key is to figure out just how far away from the bench to start. You want your seat to make contact with the bench and to end the roll in a V-seat on the bench [demonstration]. From a V-seat on the bench, you can roll halfway over onto the tummy. From there you can place your hands on the floor, slide your tummy and thighs off the bench, transferring your weight into a roll, and finish on the floor. Begin by experimenting with three ways to use a slide, rock, or roll to approach, mount, travel on, and dismount the bench or box. If you need to, use the mat to provide cushioning on the benches. If you are trying something new or something you are not sure about, ask me or a partner to spot for your safety. [The idea of spotting should be introduced early in gymnastics. It is a way to help someone who is doing a new or difficult skill. Children should be taught how to spot for different skills so they can help each other.] Finish by making a short sequence—balance position, weight transfer, and new balance. Your choices include

- balance off the equipment, weight transfer to arrive, balance on the equipment
- balance on the equipment, weight transfer to dismount, balance off the equipment
- balance on the equipment, weight transfer on the equipment, balance on the equipment

"Work hard at developing your sequence. Practice it several times until you can remember it exactly. You want to eliminate all the bugs or glitches. There should be no extra hand movements, weight shifts, or extra steps. After you've practiced, show your sequence to a partner. Watch your partner's sequence, and then tell them one thing you really liked about their work. See if their rock, roll, or slide was fast or slow. Did they make a smooth transition from one balance to the next? Did they transfer weight onto or off the equipment smoothly? After sharing, put away the equipment and line up at the door."

Look For

- Weight transfer to enable the body to move short distances and to change positions (see Figure 6.4) when the weight transfers from one adjacent part to the next.
- Rocking and rolling actions executed with the attention focused on making the body parts smooth and rounded.
- Weight transfer actions from one balance to another that enable smooth transitions and eliminate unneeded steps, extra arm or leg gestures (glitches), pauses, and stops.

How Can I Change This?

- Make up the weight transfer sequence entirely on the floor: for example, balance—weight transfer—balance—weight transfer—balance.
- Use weight transfer as traveling to make a longer, more complete sequence: for example, balance—move to arrive—mount—balance—move on—balance—move to dismount—balance.
- Make up a simple weight transfer sequence performed with a partner either on or off the equipment.
- More able children might try a handstand with a lowering, rocking action onto the chest, tummy, and thighs into a front support (fish flop). Using the same fish flop, they could move out of a backward exit to a shoulder stand. The key is in timing and arching the back to get a nicely curved (concave) surface on which to rock.

TEACHABLE MOMENTS

Show the children the inside workings of a clock or simple machine. Point out how cogs mesh and pistons slide. Movement is smooth. Weight transfer from one adjacent part to the next helps the performance of the machine. In the same way weight transfer helps the body travel from one position to another.

Talk about dance fads, such as break dancing, the moon walk, or body wave, as examples of ways people transfer weight. Although allowing children to spin on their heads is dangerous, without that break dancing is an excellent example of weight transfer from one body part to another being smooth and continuous.

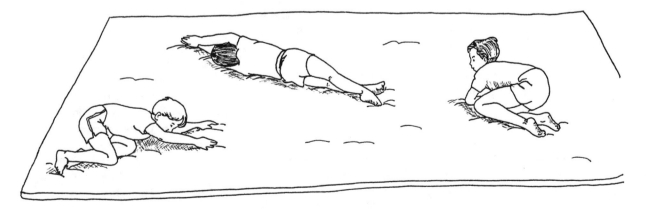

Figure 6.4 Rocking, rolling, twisting, and other weight transfer actions are a means of traveling into new body positions.

FANTASY FLIGHT

Objectives

As a result of participating in this learning experience, children will improve their ability to

- vault onto and off of selected equipment
- demonstrate a variety of shapes in the air and land safely
- experience flight through the air as high and as far as possible
- perform a linked movement sequence that includes a vault, roll, and balance (5-6, #4)

Suggested Grade Range

Primary (2–3)

Organization

Benches and boxes are scattered around gym. Mats are arranged safely around the equipment.

Equipment Needed

1 hoop for each student for the warm-up; mat, box, bench, and vaulting box also are needed for every 2-3 students.

Description

"Let's start moving! Start running slowly around the mats. Be careful not to run into anyone. Pick up the speed. OK, when you hear me clap, change your speed, choosing either slow, medium, or fast as you travel around the gym. Clap. Clap . . . clap. Now, everyone run at medium speed and when you come near someone, jump up and give that person a double high five. Keep going; find a new partner. Use your arms and legs to jump as high as you can. Stop.

"Find a hoop on the floor, pick it up, and use it to stretch your body different ways. I like the way Ashley and Davey are moving in and out of the hoop to stretch their bodies. Really stretch your muscles and enjoy the feeling. Yes, Kelly, you can also sit or lie on the floor as you stretch with the hoop.

"Today, the main part our lesson is work on flight and on vaulting. You'll travel around the room, and when you come to a bench or a box, jump onto and then off of it. Use a hurdle or spring takeoff to jump onto the bench [demonstrate]. Swing your arms up to jump as high as you can on your rebound jump off the bench; land and keep going. Any questions? OK, go! [Give reminders during practice.] Keep your body tall. Good jump. Reach higher. Can you jump one body length high? Very good. And stop.

"Now when you jump off a bench, make a neat shape in the air, and still land on two feet. Try to make as many different shapes as you can. Go. Nice! I see a tuck with knees to the chest. Nicki's doing a star with her arms and legs stretched out. Jeremy's doing a pike with straight legs forward. Good, I see a straddle with legs spread out, and even symmetrical and asymmetrical shapes. Stop.

"Let's work on making better landings. *Squash* as you land, bending your hips, knees, and ankles. This will help you keep a soft, balanced landing [demonstrate]. Go. [During practice] Keep your hands off the floor when you land. Land on the balls of your feet, not your heels. Much better. Squash! [Pinpoint several examples of good jumps and landings.] Stop. This time, move into a roll as you land from each jump. Roll in whatever direction your landing takes you. [Signal start and stop.]

"Now, we are going to learn how to vault onto and off of apparatus in a variety of ways. [The ideal height for apparatus is about at the children's waist level. Using a hurdle or spring takeoff, the children should be able to land on the apparatus with the feet together between the hands, and then jump off.] For vaulting our hands arrive on the apparatus before the legs. [Be prepared to spot at the shoulders for the children, or teach them to spot for each other. Demonstration.] So, you run, vault on, land, jump off, and squash.

"Some secrets to a good vault are to get good height off the first jump and get your weight up over your hands. Keep your arms straight, your hips high, and your head up. Think of these as you practice. Go! Now, try to vault without your feet landing on the vaulting box. Bring your feet through the middle without touching [squat vault]. Great. After you take your turn vaulting over the box, turn and move to the bench. Jump onto the bench and make a shape. Then jump off, create a shape in the air, land, and roll. By the time you finish that, it will be your turn again to vault. Try to vault with your feet outside your hands in a straddle position [straddle vault]. Again, land on the vaulting box first and, when you feel confident, try to straddle vault over the vaulting box. [Demonstrate. Be prepared to spot for the children, or to teach them to spot for each other.]

"Finally let's take these vaults and link them to other actions we know. Our movement sequence today will be vault-roll-balance. Decide what movements you will use for your sequence and then practice the sequence over and over. Show the sequence to your partner.

"Stop. Everyone come in. Who can tell me the names of two vaults we learned today? What is important to do when trying to vault well? Yes, Rinji. Good hurdle jumps, with the arms straight and shoulders over the hands; good landings. What did you like best about the sequences you saw? Good, Matt—exciting vaults, shapes in the air. Yes, Marta, smooth transitions. Right, Tonya, different rolls, variety, and stillness in the final balances. You all worked hard today. That's it."

Look For

- A powerful, explosive leg thrust, the key to jumping in the air. Jump up, get height, and swing the arms up high.

- Flights in the air with clear and crisp shapes, and proper timing into and out of shapes before landing. Watch for good lines in the arms and legs and good extension through the fingers and toes.

- A good two-footed takeoff in vaulting. Jump high and place hands on the vaulting box. Keep the arms straight, shoulders over the hands, hips high (see Figure 6.5). By placing the majority of weight over the arms, the legs are left free to do their work.

How Can I Change This?

- Try additional types of vaults: both legs over same side (flank vault); one leg through the middle, one to the side (wolf vault); with a quarter or half turn to face a new direction.

- In the absence of a vaulting box, travel to a bench or smaller box. Jump onto the box and rebound-jump into the air. Make a shape in the air, land, roll, and balance.

Figure 6.5 Children should vault onto and off of the equipment by jumping high and keeping their hips high while the shoulders, hands, and arms are aligned with one another.

TEACHABLE MOMENTS

Vaulting over objects is key to being a versatile mover. Vaults can be used to jump over a bicycle rack, fence, a fallen tree, or over children, as in leapfrog.

Vaulting and jumping actions are used in a variety of sports including pole vault, high jump, hurdles, jumping over a potential tackler in football, jumping for a rebound in basketball, and jumping for a spike in volleyball. What shape does the body create while it is in the air? a stretch, bend, pike, twist?

CLOCKFACE

Objectives

As a result of participating in this learning experience, children will improve their ability to

- use steplike actions to transfer body weight from the feet to the hands and back to the feet in a variety of ways
- develop strength in the arms and shoulder girdle (5-6, #15)
- work cooperatively with a partner in individual tasks and in the development of a partner sequence (5-6, #4)

Suggested Grade Range

Intermediate (4–6)

Organization

A large open area such as a gym floor, a stage, or a parachute on the grass is essential. Mats can be arranged in rows or columns or placed in scattered formation with adequate space between them.

Equipment Needed

1 hula hoop, a piece of chalk and 1 mat (4' × 6') for every 2 children

Description

"As we get started today, let's begin by using steplike actions around the floor. Stay off the mats. Yes, I see some of you running, others hopping, jumping, or skipping. Remember, I want good form, like a gymnast—not racing—high knees, light feet. Use the arms for lift, and think of good posture through your trunk and head. Good, I also see you're remembering to go backward and sideways, use long and short steps, and sometimes go faster or slower. Stop!

"OK. This time when you travel, approach a mat. When you get to one, lower your body, and put your hands down on the mat. Transfer your weight, changing from feet to hands to feet to hands as you travel across the mat. Then move away from the mat and travel on to another mat, using your feet and hands in a different traveling pattern to keep on going. Any questions? Go!

[After some practice] "Each time you come to a new mat, remember to do different things with your body and feet as you take weight on your hands. Stay tucked up and do bunny-hops. [Demonstrate.] Stretch out and do mule kicks. Land on one foot, the other foot, both feet. Allow your feet to come down where they started. Take your feet to your left and right sides as you twist your body. Remember, you are traveling across the mat, so your hand and foot placements should take you somewhere. I also should see you land softly each time on your feet—no crashing! Try it one more time. [Signal start and stop.] Come on over to me.

"Good warm-up! Now we are ready for the main part of the lesson: taking weight on our hands using a clockface. Everyone will have a partner to work with cooperatively. When you're at your mat, use a piece of chalk or the hula hoop to create a clockface. Draw numbers on the mat from 1 to 12. Then you'll be ready to start. I'll explain what you'll be doing after I have a volunteer to help me demonstrate [choose student].

"You and your partner will take turns. One will be the performer while the other is the observer. The observer will call out times and positions for the performer to start and finish in. [Post the progressions on a bulletin board, if you wish.] The observer also will give the performer some hints to help him or her do better.

"Start each movement with a long, thin (pencil) stretch, standing on a number at the edge of the clock. You'll all begin at the number six [student demonstrates the following movements]. Your arms should be extended straight over the head; from here, lean or topple forward. This will throw your center of gravity outside your base of support, and you'll begin to lose your balance. So, take a small step or lunge forward; bend forward and place your hands on the ground in the center of the clock. The trail leg—the one in the back—kicks up with the leg straight and tight, then lands softly back on the same foot, in this case on the number six again. So, the sequence goes stretch—topple—lunge—kick up. Let's watch Jenny do this all together. She starts at number six, stretches, topples, lunges, kicks up. Notice she kicked up with only a small amount of force. Do this sequence until you can control your kick. If you kick up high and control it for a long time, what do you think you're doing? Yes, Zachary, a handstand!

"Now, the observer should be looking for two important hints. Are your partner's arms always straight, and when they lunge, is their knee right over the front foot? As Jenny tries it one more time, everyone notice if her arms are straight and where her knee is when she lunges. If she needed some help, the observer could tell her which of those she needs to work on. Remember, while you're the observer, you will also give the different numbers to start and finish on. After two tries at each number, switch roles. OK? Any questions? If not, go ahead. Get a partner, go to a mat, and begin.

[During practice] "Remember that as you are using the clockface, you are developing arm strength and body control and using steplike actions to transfer weight from the feet to hands to feet. Observers, check to see if your partner's arms are straight, and if their knee is over their foot.

"Do these progressions:

- Start at 6, take weight on hands, return to 6.
- Start at 6, return to 5 or 7.
- Start at 6, return to 4 or 8, increasing the angle of rotation.
- Start at 6, return to 6 after changing the landing leg (scissors in air). Come down on both feet.
- Partner call position: 6 to 8, 8 to 5, 4 to 7.
- Move the hand positions around the center to allow greater rotation: 6 to 10, 6 to 2, 6 to 11, 6 to 1, 6 to 12.
- For the very able who can pirouette, reduce the radius of the clockface. Get the feet close to the hands.

"Stop. Everyone gather around and sit down. Today we worked very hard at using several ways to transfer body weight from the feet to hands to feet, using various steplike actions. This helps develop arm strength and control. As we get better and better, we should be able to use these actions to build sequences individually, or with a partner. We'll work on that in future lessons. That's it for now."

Look For

- During the second part of the warm-up, children should use mats and floor spaces interchangeably. It is important to move to open spaces and take turns, rather than wait in long lines.

- Stress good mechanics and control during practice. Focus children's efforts on straight arms, knee over foot, and tight bodies (Figure 6.6). Careful work now pays dividends later in more sophisticated sequence work.

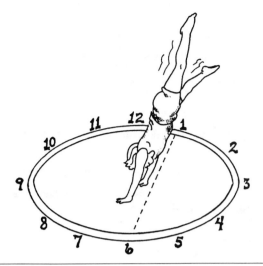

Figure 6.6   Take weight on the hands using the clockface.

How Can I Change This?

- For developing arm strength an interesting variation on the clockface is for the children to put their feet in the center and walk their hands around to the times while in push-up position.

- Once children develop control in taking weight on their hands, they should be encouraged to use these steplike actions of transferring weight from feet to hands to feet in sequence work. Two examples follow that include a partner. During these two partner sequences play music in the background. Children enjoy choreographing their work to music.

- Sequence work with a partner:

  Lead-follow. One partner puts together a short sequence that the other partner copies or repeats. For example, jump or hop three times to arrive at the mat (considering the direction, turns, and time); stretch; topple; lunge; return to one foot or two feet; lower into a rolling action of your choice; and finish in a balance of your choice.

  Partners moving simultaneously. Perform a sequence similar to the lead-follow one, with an emphasis on partner relationships. Partners mirror or match each other while moving face-to-face or side-by-side.

> **TEACHABLE MOMENT**
>
> Partner work may start with students calling out clockface position. Begin to place an emphasis on partners giving feedback to each other on performance. Have them talk to a partner about what they observe in arm and leg positions, soft landings, and hand placement, if necessary. This gives them responsibility to assist with instruction, improve cognitive awareness, and increase their aesthetic perception.

BEAM ME UP

Objectives

As a result of participating in this learning experience, children will improve their ability to

- demonstrate proper use of undergrip, overgrip, and mixed grip
- perform a movement sequence that involves a rising action, roll, and balance starting under a large piece of apparatus (5-6, #4)

Suggested Grade Range

Intermediate (5–6)

Organization

A large open space is needed with mats arranged safely under each piece of apparatus. Add additional mats so children can create movement sequences away from the equipment.

Equipment Needed

1 or more of the following large pieces of apparatus is needed: balance beams, horizontal bars, or parallel bars. In this lesson, students will be working under the equipment, so as many as 4 children can use a piece of equipment at a time. At least 3 pieces of equipment would be ideal, but you can adapt to whatever situation you have. In addition to placing mats under the equipment, at least 2 mats leading to and away from each piece of apparatus are needed to provide space for sequence work, maximize safety, and give multiple opportunities for practice.

Description

"As you can see, today we are going to be using large equipment. It's going to be a challenging class! But before we start working on the equipment, we need to warm up properly. Find a space on a mat and lie down in your space. Make yourself as tall as you can. *Really* stretch. Pretend one person is pulling your arms, and another person is pulling your legs at the same time. Now make your body as wide as you can: imagine that there is one person on each arm and leg pulling sideways at the same time out from your body. Next, curl your body into a tight ball. Relax into a long stretch again. Repeat these in a sequence three times very slowly on your own: long, wide, curl.

[When done] "Now, start in a long sit and reach your arms toward your toes. Hold this position and count 10 to 15 seconds. Enjoy the stretch in your lower back, and feel it in your hamstrings. Now rock back into a shoulder stand, and stretch your legs wide and like a scissors. Come down into a straddle-seat position, place one hand behind your back and lift your body into the air, stretching the free arm into the air. Your body weight should be on the one hand behind your back and your feet. Relax. Now, link these three actions together three times at a slow, stretching speed: long sit–shoulder stand–straddle. Try this on your own. [Signal stop.]

"Now, when I say go, move over to the beams, parallel bars, or horizontal bar. There should be no more than four of you to a balance beam or two to a set of parallel bars or horizontal bar. If necessary, you can double up and take turns with a partner. Go. [When situated] Wherever you are, sit directly under the equipment, so the beam or bar is over your head. Using the adjustment knobs, set the beam or bar at a height where each of your arms can reach up to grasp it as you stretch comfortably. Sit in alternating directions so you are facing opposite the person next to you. This will allow you to move in opposite directions without interfering with each other.

"First we'll go over grasp positions with our hands. You should all be able to do this at the same time. Reach up and grasp the bar or beam with both palms facing back to you (thumbs out). This is called an *undergrasp*. Reach up and grasp the bar or beam with both palms facing away from you (thumbs in). This is called an *overgrasp*. Reach up and grasp the beam or bar with one palm facing toward you, and one facing away. This is called a *mixed grasp*. [Demonstrate.] Ready? Show me mixed . . . over . . . under. Right! You've got them.

"Now we want to do something with these grasps. Watch me demonstrate. Sitting directly under your equipment, you'll use a mixed grasp. Pull, then push your body with a twist as you make a quarter turn and rise up to two knees [demonstrate]. Your arms end up crossing as you rise to a kneeling position. The sequence is pull—twist—knees. You can only go in one direction to make this work; see if you can figure it out. Take turns if you need to. Also, try the opposite mixed grasp and rise to your knees facing the opposite direction. [After repeated practice] Try the same move, but make a half turn as you rise to your knees. Try it in the opposite direction, too.

"Next, I want you to use the mixed grasp with a quarter or half turn and rise up to a knee and a foot. Now use an undergrasp, and try to pull through and rise to a standing position facing away from the bar or beam. This is called a *body wave*. Pull through—wave—feet. [As the arms thrust up and back, the chest should lead the body into an erect, standing position over the feet. After repeated practice]

"All of these rising actions are the same as when you resolve the shoulder stand. They put you in a position to decide what comes next. Rising to two knees allows you to rock back into a shoulder stand. Rising to one knee and foot gives you an easy exit into a cartwheel. A rise to two feet allows movement into steplike actions. With any of this work you can either move away from or back toward the bar or beam for continuous actions and sequence work. Let's try some of these combinations, starting with the rise to two knees, then rocking back into a shoulder stand. Practice this on your own as I travel around to watch and help. [Follow with other combinations.]

"Let's end the class by developing a short sequence. Perform a rising action of your choice. Take that into a shoulder stand, roll, cartwheel, or steplike action—away from or back toward the bar or beam. Finish in a balance position on the floor or on the bar or beam. Practice your sequence over and over until you can do it smoothly. Show your sequence to a partner.

"Stop. Everyone come in. Who can tell me the names of the three hand positions on the equipment that we learned today? When you started those positions, where were you? Right, Bill, sitting under the bar or beam in a long sitting position. As you moved out of the gymnast-sit, what did you do? Yes, Li, you transferred your body weight to two feet, a knee and a foot or to two knees. That movement created a smooth transition so you could go on and link one action to another to create a sequence. This is difficult work, and you are doing very well.

Look For

- Are the children using the proper grasp (as in Figure 6.7)?

- Are the children using good body lines? Rising actions should bring the body to erect positions (Figure 6.8). Watch for tight bodies. A rise to two knees should have the hips over the knees, for example, and there should be no sagging bottoms. See that a rise to a knee and a foot includes the hips over the kneeling leg, with the leading knee over the foot. A rise using the body wave action should start from a long sitting position with the body erect and directly under the bar or beam, ending with body over feet.

- Are the actions in the sequence linked together smoothly with one action leading into the next?

Figure 6.7   The bars can be grasped with the hands in three different ways.

Figure 6.8   Children can also rise from the bars or beam in a number of different ways.

How Can I Change This?

- Add such work to the sequence as a support position, on top of the beam, straddle over the beam, or rotation around the beam.
- Combine work on top and around the beam with work under the beam to create movement sequences.
- Add equipment such as benches or boxes to use for travel away from the beam and toward other pieces.

TEACHABLE MOMENTS

Show the children some gymnastics routines on beams or bars. Use Olympic performers' tapes or videos from your previous classes. Relate the taped sequencing to their routines. Every routine has a beginning, middle, and end—a mount, some actions, and a dismount. The children do a rise, an action, and a balance.

Using good body mechanics helps the flow in all actions. The pull-up in the rising actions raises the center of gravity over a new base (knees and feet). The rise can lead into a shoulder stand, steplike action, or wheeling action. Just like the pendulum of a clock, the rising action on one end of a swing is used to establish the momentum for the following downward action. One movement leads to the next in smooth transition.

ME AND MY SHADOW

Objectives

As a result of participating in this learning experience, children will improve their ability to

- explore the relationships of meeting and parting, leading and following, and mirroring and matching
- experience the adaptation and responsibility necessary to work with another person (5-6, #27)
- develop a linked sequence of travel-balance-travel with a partner (5-6, #4)

Suggested Grade Range

Intermediate (5–6)

Organization

A large open space is needed with mats spread out so that children can travel between them.

Equipment Needed

1 mat for every 2 children is ideal.

Description

"Today, you will be working with a partner. Quickly sit next to someone by the time I count to five. 1, 2, 3, 4, 5. We are going to work especially hard at different relationships you can have with your partner. We'll start by playing follow the leader to warm up. Which partner will lead? follow? You choose. The leader may choose to run, jump, hop, skip, or whatever on the floor. When you arrive at a mat, choose a roll, cartwheel, or some other action. Go.

[During warm-up] "Remember to change pathways and directions. Start rather slowly, so your follower can remember what you do. A good leader watches out of the corner of their eye to make sure the follower can keep up. If you're ready, you can speed up, slow down, try turns, spins, jumps with a shape in air: you choose. Keep working hard. Good, I see people doing jumps with quarter and half turns, skips, pencil rolls, even a shoulder roll to a knee and a foot rise. Stop. Now, whoever was the follower becomes the leader. Work hard at staying with your partner. Stay close to your partner and anticipate any changes in their traveling. Try a skip forward to slide sideways. Yes, Felipe! You were very alert that time. Stop; move to a mat with your partner.

"Next, you are going to work at mirroring your partner's movement *while* you're both moving. *Mirroring* means that you copy someone exactly, as though there is a reflection (as in a mirror) [explain: right to left]. Right now, decide who will be the leader and who will be the mirror. [When done] OK, you'll start in a stationary position, face-to-face with your partner. The leader will slowly change arm and leg positions to create different body shapes. Make some shapes symmetrical and some asymmetrical. Some should be at high levels, others at lower levels. Work at changing shapes so well together that I can't tell who is leading and who is following. Go. [After some practice] Try some traveling actions while you mirror each other. Use hops and jumps. While you're still mirroring each other, move to meet and part. Be sure to switch roles. Stop.

"Now, we are going to work at matching our partner's movement. *Matching* means that you are doing the *exact same* thing as your partner. This is the opposite of mirroring, it is right side to right side. We'll try this by working on a sequence I give you with a specific number of counts. First, let's see if we can all do four counts together. I'll lead. The counts will be hop left, hop left, jump forward to a two-foot straddle, turn halfway around clockwise. Ready? Do it with with me: Hop, hop, jump, turn. Again! Hop, hop, jump, turn. Make sure we're all together. Again. Hop, hop, jump, turn. Great. You're getting the idea. Now, with your partner at a mat, create your own eight-count sequence. You may choose to be front-back or side-by-side. You may choose any combination of locomotor actions or even use a roll or cartwheel. Experiment for two minutes to choose the eight actions you want to sequence. [During practice] Now work hard at your timing. Make sure you are together. You should look like moving shadows. Good work! [Signal stop.]

"For the final challenge today we are going to build a sequence, adding some new choices. The sequence will be an eight-count travel, a balance, and another eight-count travel with your partner. Your new choices can include meeting and parting, mirroring, and matching. For example, as partners you could start away from each other, off the mat. You could use the first eight counts to hop, hop, jump-turn a quarter clockwise, slide, slide, slide, jump-turn a quarter counter clockwise, and jump straddle. During these eight counts you might be moving together to arrive on the mat; you'd be meeting. [Demonstrate.] Next, you could choose a symmetrical or an asymmetrical balance [demonstrate]. Finally you could use eight more counts to travel away from each other; so you'd be parting. During this whole sequence you will either choose to mirror, right to left, or match, right to right, your partner's movements.

"The key is choosing traveling actions and a balance you can do with your partner. You and your partner will have to make a lot of decisions. This will challenge you to work hard. Remember, travel-balance-travel. Once you have decided on the actions and order of the sequence, practice it over and over until you are ready to present it to another set of partners.

[After repeated practice] "As we end today let's pretend we are at the Olympics. You are going to perform your partner sequence for another set of partners who haven't seen your routine yet. I will give you a 3 × 5 card, and you are to judge the sequence of your partners on a six-point scale [see the appendix]. Two points will be for your choice of traveling actions. You must show variety: steplike and a roll or cartwheel, for example. Two points will be for your choice of balance position. Two points will be for how well you mirror or match your partner. In addition, you must write on your card one sentence that tells something that you liked about the sequence you judged."

Look For

- Accurate timing of the partner actions (see Figure 6.9). Moving with someone while mirroring or matching is hard. Silent counting, a blink, and so on may be used as signals to start, change direction, or move into a balance.

- Challenging tasks. Are the children working at an appropriate level of difficulty?

- Good quality in performing the actions, including good extensions through the arms and legs, good eye focus, and good awareness of all body parts.

How Can I Change This?

- Use simple equipment like ropes, hoops, or wands to develop partner sequences.

- Use a piece of apparatus to develop more complex partner sequences (see Figure 6.10). Move to the apparatus, balance on, travel away. Use other choices for the ending sequence such as to start away from the mat, but move sideways to meet at the mat, or to start side by side and move together to arrive at the mat.

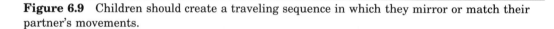

Figure 6.9   Children should create a traveling sequence in which they mirror or match their partner's movements.

Figure 6.10   To change this learning experience children can create a traveling sequence that mirrors or matches their partner's movements on equipment.

TEACHABLE MOMENT

Relate this work to the precision marching of a drill team, marching band, or a cheerleading squad. Mirroring and matching others requires concentration, cooperation, teamwork, and discipline.

Chapter 7

Learning Experiences for Statics

This chapter includes eight learning experiences within the skill theme of statics. LEs have been developed for the three categories of statics, which include characteristics, principles, and types of balance. The following outline provides a quick glance at the focus and suggested grade range for each learning experience.

Focus	Name	Suggested grade range
Characteristics of balances: stillness, control, tightness	Patches and Points	Pre-K–2
Principles of balance: base of support, center of gravity	Push and Pull	1–2
Types of balances: symmetrical and asymmetrical	Same, Different	1–2
Types of balances: inverted	Shoulder Stand	2–3
Types of balances: inverted	Bottoms Up	3–4
Types of balances: hangs, supports	Just Hanging Around	4–5
Types of balances: various types in relationship to equipment	See What I Can Do	5–6
Principles and types of balances: counter-tension and counter-balance, relationship to partner	Lean On Me	5–6

PATCHES AND POINTS

Objectives

As a result of participating in this learning experience, children will improve their ability to

- balance on a variety of large and small body parts, using characteristics of good form (1-2, #7)
- name several classic gymnastics balances and invent solutions to balance problems
- develop a simple balance sequence: balance—weight transfer—balance

Suggested Grade Range

Primary (Pre-K–2)

Organization

A large open space is needed with mats arranged in scatter formation. Children should spread out in personal space using the mats.

Equipment Needed

Mats—1 for every 2 children

Description

"Today we will begin with an easy jog. Pick your knees up. Move quietly, on light feet. When I say freeze, make a *wide* shape. Freeze! Go again. When I say freeze, make a *narrow* shape. Freeze. [Repeat several times, using a variety of shapes.] Now travel, using your feet very, very quickly and then very, very slowly. When you come to a mat, jump across it with two feet. Try long jumps. Good—now short, quick jumps. Now skip while you travel between the mats. Lift your knees high, and push your toes into the floor. Stop. This time, when you come to a mat, lower yourself slowly into a long, tight, narrow shape like a pencil [demonstrate, lying down with the arms over the head]. Roll across the mat. Get up and skip on to the next mat. Ready? Go. [Repeat several times.]

"Now that we are warmed up, I want you to get with a partner and sit on a mat so you are facing me. Let's all sit in our gymnast-sit. That's right—legs together, toes pointed, body tall, arms at your sides. We also call this a long sitting position. Let's quickly do some other positions. [Review tuck, front support (push-up), back support, shoulder stand, straddle standing, and straddle front support.] Now I'll call out the names, and you move from one position to the next. Ready—front support—tuck—back support—long sit—shoulder stand—tuck. . . .

"Today we are working on balancing in different positions. Some of the positions have names. Others don't. We will be using different body parts to *balance*. Can you name some body parts we have already used? [Feet, hands, seat, shoulders.]

"Let's begin to call the smaller body parts we use to balance *points*. Our larger body surfaces let's call *patches*. Can you name some points? [Hands, feet, elbows, knees, head.] Can you name some patches? [Seat, shoulders, tummy, thigh, forearm, shin.] On your mats, let's see if we can balance on some of these patches and points. I'll get you started. How about your right forearm and right thigh [free leg up—straddled]?

How about your seat and two hands [legs in pike or straddle position]? How about your tummy [back arched, arms out]? Now balance on one knee and the opposite hand, the hand on your other side.

"Now I'll give you some choices. Figure them out. Balance on one patch and two points. On four points. Three points. Two points. One patch and one point. Can you make a wide balance, [then narrow balance] using patches? points? Can you make a balance where your head is lower than your hips?

"Now comes the fun part. Let's see how to put two balances together into a sequence. A sequence has a beginning and ending with action in between. Make sure you hold your beginning balance until you can count to 3. The beginning balance is a signal to say watch me, I'm ready to start. I want you to show me stillness—that you have control. Then move into your second balance. Hold your second balance until you can count to 3. It says, I am finished. Choose one balance, move smoothly out of that balance into a new one. [For example, shoulder stand with legs straddled, rolling-rocking down into a V-seat with hands supporting.] You don't have to move much to get into a new balance. You can use a rolling, rocking, sliding, or steplike action with the hands or feet to move smoothly into your second balance.

"Let's see you try different balances on patches and points, and smoothly link them to your second balance. Make up your favorite sequence [balance—transfer—balance] and practice it several times to make it look really good. [Note: If appropriate, encourage students to make two sequences. In one sequence, they make the transfer fast: balance—quick action—another balance. In another, they make their transfer very slowly: balance—move slowly out of that balance into the second balance.] Make sure you hold your balances until you count to 3 to show control, with a good beginning and ending. Then find a partner and show them your sequence [after repeated practice].

"Stop. Everyone come in here and sit down. Quick. Who can tell me the name of one of the balances we did today? Right, Molly, front support. Yes, Rinji, squat. Good, Billy, V-sit. We also invented some that didn't have names, didn't we? What does it take to balance well? Yes, Kaitlin, your body tight. Good, José, stillness, counting to 3 for control. You are already becoming good gymnasts."

Look For

- Are the children conscious of good form? While ability levels vary and children will try easier or harder balances (see Figure 7.1), everyone should do well whatever they choose: Check to see good bases, alignment, support, lines, tight bodies, and control (holding for 3 seconds).

- When appropriate, focus on good transition movements or linking actions. The children should work to remove extra steps, glitches, and unnecessary movements. Often a short step, a twist, a turn, or a movement from one adjacent body part to the next is the best way to get smooth weight transfer.

How Can I Change This?

- Make up a visual symbol for different body parts (hand, foot, large oval for seat, circle for head; see the appendix). Make a series of visual charts or posters for different balances. Play a game holding up one chart, then another, getting the children to solve the visual balance puzzles, one after another.

- More advanced learners can try longer sequences. For example, they might link three balances with two transitions: balance—move—balance—move—balance.

Figure 7.1   Basic balance positions.

TEACHABLE MOMENTS

Have the children name the classic gymnastic balance positions, increasing their movement vocabulary. Show them pictures of Olympic gymnasts.

Help the children analyze their balances. Which are most stable? Which are least stable? Why? Talk about what makes a good balance.

PUSH AND PULL

Objectives

As a result of participating in this learning experience, children will improve their ability to

- vary the number of body parts they use as bases of support for balancing with good form (1-2, #7)
- identify factors that make some balances more stable than others
- work cooperatively with a partner to determine stable balance positions
- develop a simple balance sequence: balance—weight transfer—balance

Suggested Grade Range

Primary (1–2)

Organization

A large open space is needed with mats arranged in scatter formation. Children should spread out in personal space, using the mats.

Equipment Needed

Mats or carpet squares—1 for every 2 children; one 3" × 5" note card and pencil for each child

Description

"Today we will work on choosing good balance positions. We'll start with a warm-up. I want to see everyone skipping around on the floor. Stay off the mats. Show me your best skip: high knees, light, springy feet, and up on the balls of your feet. I see arms swinging, too. Good! Change speeds—try slow, now faster. OK, change directions— forward, sideways, backward. Skip while you turn or spin around. Stop. Watch me. This time skip, and as you get close to a mat, jump and land on two feet. Lower your body to the mat and roll. Finish your roll by coming to your feet. OK? [Signal start.] Keep going—skip, jump, land, roll. Stop.

"Now that we are warmed up, find a partner you know you can work with, and sit down beside a mat. Today we are going to learn why some balances are stronger or more stable than others. You and your partner will take turns balancing and helping. When it is your turn to balance, do the best you can. When you are the helper, you will help by questioning and by *gently* pushing your partner from one way to another. I'll show you what I mean as we get started. Now, decide who will balance first. They should choose two body parts to balance on. I see several of you have chosen two feet. That is a good way to begin. Let's watch here. Ashley is just standing, two feet together. What if I were to face her and gently push her from the shoulder [demonstrate]? Yes, she would fall over. OK, what if you stand with your feet wide apart? [Have a student demonstrate.] If I push gently from the side, you are strong—you don't fall over. But, if I push you from the front or back, it's easy to lose your balance. So, how could we make a standing balance the most stable—so you won't fall over? See if you and your partner can figure out a way. One partner can gently push. I'll give you a hint. You may need to make your body or feet look *different* than what we just did. Try this now, and make sure both you and your partner get a chance. [Stop.]

"I saw some of you get a good balance by bending to get lower, moving your feet apart into a stride or straddle position, and making a wide base [demonstrate]. These ideas help set strong balances. But gymnasts rarely stay standing still, except when they're done with a routine. So, let's try some balances on two other body parts besides the feet. How about a hand and a foot? Your seat and hand? Show me another balance you think of. Of all these, which do you think is the most stable? Show this one to your partner now, and talk with your partner about why you think it's the most stable. Then watch their balance and listen while they tell you why they think it's a very strong balance. [After some time] What answers did you discuss?

"Yes, Li, your body being low; OK, Kelly, a wide base and staggered feet or body parts can all help make your balance strong and stable. Now, let's try the same types of balances but use two [three, four, or more] bases of support for the balances. Take turns with your partner. See which way is most stable and strong by having your partner gently push you when you have made a balance and are ready. Which balances are most stable? Why? Remember, choose good gymnastics balances. I want to see good balances—think of what every part of your body is doing. [During practice] Remember, the more bases of support you have, the more stable your balance is. When your body is low and your base is wide you have better balance. I want to see good, strong muscles. Tighten your muscles—no wobbly, loose bodies. Keep your eyes looking at one place to help you hold your balance while you count to 3. OK, Stop.

"Sometimes gymnasts use a balance to take them into their next move. They may stretch, bend, or lean in one direction or another until they feel their body topple or fall. Then they step, twist, turn, or roll to regain their balance. The good gymnast is always in control. Let's all try this. Choose a balance. Hold it. Now lean or topple. Lose your balance, but move into a new balance. Go ahead and try different ways to balance. Choose one you like and practice it several times. Balance—transfer—balance. Then watch your partner. Tell them why they made good choices from what you know now about good balance positions.

"OK. Everyone in. I am going to give everyone a [3" × 5"] card and a pencil. Before you leave class for today I want you to write down one or more ideas that help you balance well [see chapter 5, Figure 5.6]. Leave your cards and pencils in the box at the door as you line up to leave."

Look For

- Children may be tempted to see who is the strongest and push each other out of balance. The purpose of the helper is to push gently, offer resistance, and yet allow the performer to succeed at the balance. The goal is for the children to discover good principles for balance.

- Children should be challenging themselves as gymnasts. Standing, kneeling, or lying down flat may be stable positions, but these are not aesthetic, challenging balances that gymnasts would choose. Keep children focused on quality work (see Figure 7.2).

Figure 7.2 Children's balances should incorporate quality principles.

How Can I Change This?

- Add a range of levels. Choose balances on one to four bases at a high, medium, or low level.
- Add the factor of extensions—wide and narrow, using different bases.
- Add different body shapes, using a different number of bases.

TEACHABLE MOMENTS

Bring in such objects as a pencil, pyramid, tall vase, and wide bowl and talk about their stability. Is a pencil more stable when standing on end or lying on its side? Why? Is a tall vase or wide bowl more stable? Why?

Examine preparatory positions for sports: track start; linebacker, offensive lineman, defensive lineman in football; infielder in baseball; swim start; and so on. Which are most stable? Why? Why do you suppose these readiness positions are used?

SAME, DIFFERENT

Objectives

As a result of participating in this learning experience, children will improve their ability to

- balance in a variety of selected symmetrical and asymmetrical shapes (1-2, #7)
- develop a simple sequence that includes a balance—travel—and balance (1-2, #17)

Suggested Grade Range

Primary (1–2)

Organization

A large open space is needed. Children should spread out, with 2 children to a mat.

Equipment Needed

1 mat for every 2 children if possible; otherwise, carpet squares or a large parachute can be used for balances.

Description

"Today's lesson is about using our body symmetrically and asymmetrically. Those are big words. Do you know what *symmetry* means? It means that both sides of your body look alike or are doing the same thing. See if you can move by making your body work symmetrically. Yes, jumping from two feet to two feet is symmetrical. Try short, quick jumps; now do long, powerful jumps. How about going from feet together to feet apart jumps? Can you think of other ways to move symmetrically? Good, Zachary, bunny-hops! Two feet, two hands forward and backward. I see some children doing forward and backward rolls. Great! Now, what about moving *asymmetrically*? This means the two sides are different. Yes, a hop is asymmetrical: One foot is on the floor and the other is up. Running is alternating feet; skipping is too. Try lots of other ways. Go fast and slow. Try moving forward, backward, sideways. Move with straight and curved pathways, too.

"Now that we are warmed up, let's sit on the mat in a long sitting position. Arms are at our sides. Are we symmetrical or asymmetrical? Yes, symmetrical. Now put your arms out to the sides parallel to the floor. Are they still symmetrical [same]? Try a V-seat. Is this symmetrical or asymmetrical? Yes, a V-seat is still symmetrical. How could we change this? Yes, Latasha, we could bend or stretch one arm or leg in a different position to make our body asymmetrical. Now do the same experiment from a front support, back support, and bridge position. Start symmetrical. Move one or two arms or legs to make your body asymmetrical. I'm going to come around and watch as you change your shapes.

"Try other balance shapes with different bases. Let me see you start symmetrical and change to asymmetrical. You can also start asymmetrical and change to symmetrical. Show me how you would do this. I want to see a definite asymmetrical shape that moves smoothly into a symmetrical shape. Nice job, Bill! You too, Marta.

"Now let's put this into a sequence. Choose a symmetrical balance. Hold it still. Add a traveling action, steplike or rolling. Finish in an asymmetrical balance. Try it several ways. Then choose your favorite combination. Practice now until it is your best work.

"Finally, let's do just the opposite sequence. Start in an asymmetrical balance and change into a symmetrical balance by a good weight transfer or steplike action. As you work on the sequence, think about how you use your time. Can you change the balance quickly? slowly? Which do you like best? Whatever you choose, practice it several times. Show your sequence to a partner.

"Stop. Everyone gather here. Sit down. Who can tell me what the word symmetrical means? Yes, same on both sides. What were some examples of symmetrical balances? Yes, a V-seat could be one. What does the word asymmetrical mean? Yes, it looks different on the two sides. What were some examples of asymmetrical balances? Yes, balancing on one leg. Good work today! Line up at the door by using a symmetrical traveling action."

Look For

- Stillness, which is essential in balancing. Can the children hold for 3 seconds to show control? Sample symmetrical and asymmetrical balances are shown in Figure 7.3.

- Are the changes in balances and from balances to traveling (using single steplike or weight transfer actions) logical and smooth? Are the children avoiding extra steps, glitches, and indecision? Their movements should be intentional and purposeful.

How Can I Change This?

- Keep the sequence the same (balance—travel—balance), but add a second focus to each balance. For example, balance one starts symmetrical, but through the change of an arm or leg position, it becomes asymmetrical. Balance two starts asymmetrical and changes to symmetrical.

- Lengthen the sequence. Use three balances and two travels: Balance—travel—balance—travel—balance. Ask for two symmetrical balances and one asymmetrical, or vice versa. One traveling action could be symmetrical and one asymmetrical. Traveling actions may be chosen from steplike movements on the feet, hands and feet, rocks, rolls, or sliding.

Figure 7.3   Sample symmetrical and asymmetrical balances.

TEACHABLE MOMENTS

Teach an awareness of geometric design. Create lines with the arms, legs, and trunk that are parallel or perpendicular to the floor. Bend the arms, legs, or hip at right, acute, and obtuse angles. Make curved body shapes—smooth and round.

Show pictures of gymnasts, bridges, buildings, machines, and pieces of art. Ask the children to pick out lines, angles, and designs from the pictures that illustrate symmetrical and asymmetrical body shapes.

SHOULDER STAND

Objectives

As a result of participating in this learning experience, children will improve their ability to

- demonstrate a successful shoulder stand, establishing a stable base with good alignment of the hips and legs over the base
- select a variety of ways to move smoothly into and out of the shoulder stand
- develop a movement sequence involving steplike traveling actions onto and off of a box or bench, a shoulder stand, and a resolving action that allows repetition of the sequence (1-2, #17)

Suggested Grade Range

Primary (2–3)

Organization

A large open space is needed with the children spread out two to a mat. This lesson also is manageable on a gym floor or outdoor grassy area using carpet squares or a large parachute. Mats should be arranged in scatter formation with good spacing between them, and a box or bench should be placed beside each mat.

Equipment Needed

1 mat and a bench or box for every 2 children

Description

"Today we will start with stretching and balancing. Later we'll make a sequence by moving into and out of a balance. Now, everyone get into a gymnast-sit position. Bend forward and reach for your toes. Reach and hold while you count to 15. Open back up and use the movement to rock back onto your shoulders. Hold yourself up by pushing your arms down against the floor. You can also bend your arms at the elbow and place your hands on your hips. Tighten your bottom (seat)—squeeze those buns together! Tighten your tummy and legs too. Point your toes. That's good, Jamie. Your hips should be over your shoulders and your legs straight up. OK, rock back down.

"Now, let's create a sequence. Watch as I demonstrate. You'll sit long, reach for your toes, rock back to a shoulder stand, rock out of your shoulder stand to a straddle seat, reach smoothly to your left and right legs, rock back to shoulder stand, come back down to a long sit, and push up to back support. I'll talk you through it once, then you'll try it on your own. Ready? [Go through sequence.] Start over.

"Now let's experiment with what to do with our legs in a shoulder stand. Get back up into a shoulder stand. Try these as I talk you through it. Straddle your legs and make scissors movements slowly. Feel the stretch in your lower back and the back of your legs. Let your feet come slowly down behind your head. Bend one leg, but keep the other leg straight. Write some letters of the alphabet with one leg. Try it now with two legs. Stop. Rock out of your shoulder stand to a sitting position. OK, take a rest!

"Good stretching! Now we are ready to learn more ways to come out of our shoulder stand balances. Get back into your shoulder stand. Hold your balance tight. Begin rocking back toward your feet. OK, whip your legs under you. Bend your knees, so the feet come close to your seat. First try to be *long* and *tall*, then *short* and *small*. Can you stand up—rise to your feet—without using your hands on the floor? That is one way to resolve the shoulder stand: Return to two feet. Practice it several times.

"Now get back into a shoulder stand. Watch me. You're going to twist and turn at the hips as you rock out. You'll turn partway to one side and come up on both your knees. Think long and tall, then short and small. No hands on the floor! That's right— bodies tall, hips over your knees, and shoulders over your hips.

"Now, get back into a shoulder stand. Next you'll bend one leg under and come out of the shoulder stand to one knee and your other foot. Can you come out of a shoulder stand to a *one-foot rise* to a stand? [Also have the children try using a backward shoulder roll to come to a knee and a foot or to two knees.] Try each way several times. Pick your favorite two or three ways and really get good at them.

"OK. Now we are ready to make a sequence. Start by running, hopping, or skipping around the floor. When you come to a mat, jump high, land softly, lower your body, rock back into a shoulder stand, and resolve the shoulder stand as you choose. Then return to traveling on your feet to another mat. Go ahead and repeat this several times [Signal stop]. OK, let's add the box or bench now. Travel on the floor using good running steps and jump up onto the bench/box. Do three quick bouncy jumps on both feet and then one big, explosive jump off the bench. Land softly on your feet. Lower yourself to the floor by squatting or sitting. Then rock back into a shoulder stand. Resolve it. Move off and start over. Try this now. I'm going to look for smooth sequences [pinpoint several students, if desired]. Keep the sequence the same this time, but when you are in a shoulder stand, slowly and smoothly move your legs into three different shapes. Resolve, or come out of your shoulder stand, ready to begin the sequence again and again. Practice this with your different leg positions. I'll come around and help you out with some hints.

"Stop. Everyone come in. Have a seat. Who can tell me three different ways to come out of, or resolve, a shoulder stand? Yes, Tonya, two knees; good, Ashley, a knee and a foot; right, William, a backward shoulder roll to a knee and a foot. Very good, you remembered. There are other ways, too. What are some words that help us keep good form? Yes, long and tall, short and small. You really learned a lot today. Resolving balances, such as a shoulder stand, in the ways you did today helps make smooth transitions as you move from one position or balance to another. That's all for today."

Look For

- Good momentum and timing, keys to successful resolutions of the shoulder stand. For rocking out of the shoulder stand the children should keep the body long to establish momentum/speed. Then they should make it short to establish a quick rotation for coming upright to a resolution of choice. They should learn not to use the hands to assist in pushing up (Figure 7.4).

- Good alignment, with the toes pointed and the legs straight or bent in aesthetic positions as children perform the shoulder stand, varying their leg positions. Gymnasts should always strive for good lines, shape, and form.

How Can I Change This?

- Work at one mat and a bench or box. Create a sequence that includes a traveling action to the bench, a balance completely or partially on the bench, a roll off the bench into a shoulder stand, and a resolution out of the shoulder stand into a balance of choice.

- Synchronize one of the lesson's sequences with a partner. The children mirror or match leg positions inverted in a shoulder stand.

Figure 7.4 Sample resolution of the shoulder stand.

TEACHABLE MOMENTS

For stable base in a shoulder stand, the weight should be on the shoulders and upper arms to the elbow. No weight should be on the neck or head. The shoulders and arms are strong and provide a sturdy base for support.

A good vertical alignment over the base provides stability. Hips, knees, and feet should be vertical over the elbow and shoulder base.

To resolve the shoulder stand, use rotary motion around a horizontal axis. To establish speed and momentum, stay long. To rotate quickly around the axis, tuck and get small.

BOTTOMS UP

Objectives

As a result of participating in this learning experience, children will improve their ability to

- demonstrate a variety of inverted (the head lower than the hips) balance positions with a stable base (3-4, #16)
- design a short sequence that includes an inverted balance (3-4, #26)
- identify by name some traditional inverted balances, such as the tip-up, tripod, headstand, forearm stand, and backbend
- create their own inverted balances

Suggested Grade Range

Intermediate (3–4)

Organization

A large open space is needed. Children should spread out in a scattered formation, 1 or 2 to a mat or carpet square.

Equipment Needed

1 mat or carpet square for every 1-2 students

Description

"We are going to work on balancing upside down today, but before we do we need to warm up. Let's start with some sideways movement. Slide right or left. Make good slides, up on the balls of your feet. Quick feet. Stay off the mats. Move in straight not curved pathways. Now keep going sideways but cross your feet. This is called the grapevine step: the right foot goes in front of left and then behind it [demonstrate].

"Next, move sideways anyway you choose with your feet. When you get to a mat, jump onto it—land and roll. Then get up and move off, again in a sideways direction. Ready? Give it a try! Stop. This time, do the same sequence: sideways—jump—land—roll, but end the roll in a long stretch position. From there go into a shoulder stand and stretch your legs in different ways [demonstrate]. Resolve the shoulder stand by coming to your feet and move off sideways. Then you're going to begin the sequence again. So it goes: sideways—jump—land—roll—shoulder stand—stretch—resolve. Try this now. [Signal stop.]

"A shoulder stand is one way to balance upside down that you already know. Today you will learn about balancing upside down in some different ways. One way to be upside down is to have your head lower than your hips. See if you can find a way to balance so your head is lower than your hips. Yes. I see Bill doing a backbend. I see two hands and a foot on the floor with the other foot high in the air. Good, Jessie! I see lots of creative ways you have found to balance upside down.

"Now, for the next 10 minutes I want you to try four traditional inverted balances. They are called a tip-up, tripod, headstand, and forearm stand. First, I will show them to you and give you good practice cues. Then you can practice each inverted balance at your mat [or carpet square]. A partner may help spot for you if you feel you need some help. Try only those balances you feel comfortable with and ready for.

- Tip-up—squat (your hands are at shoulder width, your elbows are out and your arms strong, your knees are on the elbows) and rock forward.

- Tripod—same as the tip-up with the forehead (hairline) on the floor. Make a triangle and keep knees on the elbows and the body tight; stay tucked.
- Headstand—same as the tripod. Your body is tight. Press the legs up and use a straight up-and-down alignment with your hips over the base and the feet and knees over your hips.
- Forearm stand—your elbows to your hands are on the floor, the forearms at shoulder width. Keep your body tight, and press up into a vertical alignment.

OK. Everyone practice. Stop.

"Now, in addition to trying these balances, see if you can invent some new balances of your own. The only rules are that you must have a good base and that your hips must be higher than your head. [Signal stop.] You sure are working hard.

"Everyone has tried several ways to balance upside down. We call that an inverted position. As gymnasts, it is important that we learn to get into and out of inverted balances smoothly. Everyone, think of an inverted balance you like and how you can practice getting into that balance smoothly. Will you roll into it? Step into it? Think of the balance as unfolding little by little. Maybe count in order—1, 2, 3, 4—to help you get it flowing. You need to get out of the balance just as smoothly as you got into it. Choose your balance and practice it now. [During practice] Always stay under control. You may want to step out lightly just the same as you got into the balance. Maybe you want to tuck and go into a roll. Try several inverted balances and work on getting into and out of each of them smoothly. [Signal stop.]

"For the last part of the lesson you'll be making up a sequence. You should do two balances of your choice. One or both of the balances can be an inverted position. Connect your two balances with whatever weight transfer you want. Balance—transfer—balance. Experiment and then choose the sequence you like best. Practice it several times so you can show it to a partner. Go! When you finish showing your work to a partner, gather in here.

"What was the main part of the lesson about today? Yes, inverted or upside-down balances. How did we define an inverted position? Right, the head lower than the hips. Using a steplike traveling action in an inverted position, move to line up at the door. OK, stand up. Walk back to your classroom."

Look For

- Correct alignment in the inverted balances (see Figure 7.5).
- In the tripod and headstand some children will align head and hands in a straight line. Point out the stability of a triangle. Check that the head is out in front of the hands.
- Children keeping tight bodies to maintain control (see Figure 7.6). If they let go from an inverted position, they will flop or crash to the floor.
- Children being able to hold balances for 3 seconds to show adequate control.
- Smooth transitions from one balance to another.

How Can I Change This?

- Combine an inverted balance with the warm-up sequence. Travel sideways to the mat, jump, land, assume inverted balance, and resolve the balance by moving back to the feet; repeat.
- Increase complexity by adding a balance. Try three balances, including at least two inverted positions. Use two different methods of weight transfer to connect the three balances.
- Perform an inverted balance sequence with a partner. Have the partners mirror or match movements. Perform side by side, face-to-face.

Back bend

Tripod

Tip-up

Headstand

Forearm stand

Figure 7.5   Inverted balances.

Figure 7.6   Children must have full control of their bodies in inverted balances.

JUST HANGING AROUND

Objectives

As a result of participating in this learning experience, children will improve their ability to

- balance in a variety of body positions on equipment, using their arms as a primary means of taking the body weight (3-4, #16)
- focus on smooth transitions to link actions, using hangs, supports, and swings on equipment in the development of a sequence
- help a partner by spotting and offering advice to improve the quality of work

Suggested Grade Range

Intermediate (4–5)

Organization

A large open space is needed with equipment well-spaced. Groups of 2 or 3 children for each piece of equipment is appropriate.

Equipment Needed

Parallel bars, horizontal bars, swinging ropes, balance beams, horses, and the like are good (outdoor playground equipment and tables may substitute for or supplement these). 1 piece of equipment should be available for every 2-3 students. Mats should be placed under and beside the equipment. Make 5 to 10 copies of Figure 7.7 for the children's use.

Description

"Gymnasts need strong arm and shoulder muscles to hang, swing, and support their body weight on all of the apparatuses. That word means more than one piece of apparatus! We'll start today in push-up position. See if you can follow my directions. Lean and balance your weight on one arm. With your free arm do a rising sun motion. At the same time turn your stomach to the ceiling into a back-support position. Turn again in the same direction to return to a push-up, which is a front-support, position.

"Now turn the other direction to return to your original push-up position on the floor. Stay in the push-up position. See if you can shoot your legs through the middle to a back-support position. Stop and listen a second. If you can't make it in one smooth move do it in two steps. Let me show you [demonstrate]. Go from front support and thrust your legs up to a squat position, with your feet between your hands. Then, thrust your legs through to a back-support position (front support—squat—back support). Practice this several times.

"Now, sit down in a long sit. Lie down. Push up into a back bend. Rock back and forth, putting most of your weight on your feet and then on your hands. If you can kick over, do a back walkover. (If you want, you can put your feet up on a folded mat, bench, or beam to help you do the back bend and back walkover.) Stop a second. As you rock, you can use this series of weight transfers to make a sequence and keep it going. It goes like this: front support—rising sun—back support—sit—lie—backbend—lower—back support—rising sun—shoot through. Add some more moves if you want. [Signal stop.]

"Get a partner, or form a group of three, and choose a piece of equipment. You can be at a swinging rope or the balance beam, parallel bars, or horizontal bar. We'll rotate, so you can get a chance at each station. The object of the lesson is to see how you can create balance shapes with your bodies in hanging, swinging, and support positions.

"I will show you some pictures [photocopy page 93]. Some of these are long stretch positions. Recognize these pike, tuck, and straddle positions? Here's an upright, and this one is inverted. Here's a symmetrical position, and this one is asymmetrical. See what you can do. Remember which grips work well for hangs and swings. How do you get good strong support positions on your arms? Shoulders over the hands; the elbows locked. Try to do 3 to 5 balance shapes from a hang, swing, or support position at your piece of equipment. Practice each shape several times. Focus on good lines and on what you're doing. Put your best effort into whatever you choose to do. [Give cues as students practice. Legs extended, toes pointed; arms parallel to the floor, your fingers stretched; tight tummy, tight bottom too are some appropriate refining comments.] I'll walk around, watch, and help. [Signal stop.] OK—rotate with your partner or group to the next piece of equipment. You may want to try the same balances at the new equipment or use different ones. Make good choices for yourself. Partners may help spot or give advice on good form. Do your best work. Think like a gymnast. Good alignment. Strong bodies. Challenging shapes. [Signal stop.]

"Rotate one more time to a new piece of equipment. Again, try some of the same balances and some new ones. Take turns and help each other.

"OK, now comes decision time. I have a feeling you were most comfortable doing balances from the hang, swing, or support position at one particular piece of equipment. You may stay with your group or change groups and go to your favorite piece of equipment. The only rule is that only two or three students may be at each place. Here's the challenge: Work at this piece and develop a short sequence. Your sequence must include three shapes with two linking actions in between. You can make shapes from hanging, swinging, or support positions or any combination of them. You can use traveling or rotation actions to link your work. For example, you might be hanging upside down on a horizontal bar or balance beam. After you hold your shape for 3 seconds, you could rotate into a back hip circle to arrive in a position of front support. From there you could create your next shape.

"Remember, three shapes and two transitions. Make your transitions or linking actions between shapes and balances as smooth as possible. When you are in a balance, think hard about how you might use a twist, turn, stretch, curl, rock, roll, step, or whatever to get smoothly to your next position. Work hard. Be helpful to your partners. Spot and give your partner ideas when necessary.

"Stop! Choose someone who is at another piece of equipment to be your partner. Use the sequences judging sheet I am handing out [see the appendix] to score or rate your partner's routine. Take turns being a performer and a judge. When it is your turn to watch, find something nice to say about your partner's routine, something that you especially liked. Talk to each other.

"Wow. I have seen some excellent sequence work today. Turn in your sheets; let's line up to leave."

Look For

- Good body mechanics for hangs, swings, and supports (see Figure 7.7); strong arms and shoulders; good alignment; tight tummies and bottoms, no sags.

- Smooth links or transitions during sequences. Use the momentum of one action to begin the next move and eliminate unnecessary movement or extra steps.

- Cooperation; compliment the children if they help and give constructive feedback to partners.

How Can I Change This?

- Change the focus of the sequence: One balance must be asymmetrical, but others symmetrical. One must be a twisted shape, but others should be stretched or curled.

Figure 7.7 Sample hangs, swings, and supports.

- Add a mount (approach) and dismount to the sequence. Traveling actions (steplike, weight transfer) and rotation actions enhance variety.
- Add a piece of equipment, such as a bench or box. The sequence might include a balance or support on the equipment; a jump, roll, or slide off the equipment; traveling or rotation actions to the second piece of equipment; and the same or a new hanging, swinging, support position.

TEACHABLE MOMENTS

Relate the previous balances on the floor to the hang, swing, and support positions taught in this lesson. How are they similar? [Long and stretched–small and tucked; wide–narrow; symmetrical–asymmetrical; upright–inverted.] Different? [Relationship to equipment is different, primarily using the arms to hang from or support body weight.]

Relate the use of mechanical principles to hanging, swinging, and support positions. When your center of gravity is over or under your base of support your body is most stable and strong. Use tricks or changes in body position at the end of a swing at the point of zero momentum to best control the action. In rotating around a piece of equipment during a transition or linking action, keep the center of gravity close to the axis of rotation to allow yourself to spin quickly.

Show videotapes of Olympic gymnastics routines on the beams, parallel bars, uneven parallel bars, rings, pommel horse, and so on. Have the children pick out supports, hangs, and swings. How are the sequences the same or different?

SEE WHAT I CAN DO

Objectives

As a result of participating in this learning experience, children will improve their ability to

- select and perform different balances on multiple pieces of equipment
- develop a sequence that involves balancing on two pieces of equipment with a smooth transition between the pieces (5-6, #4)
- work cooperatively and productively with others in sharing equipment (5-6, #27)

Suggested Grade Range

Intermediate (5–6)

Organization

A large open space is needed. Place equipment so that every 2 pieces are near each other (Figure 7.8): a box and a bench, a bench and bars, a horse and a box, and so forth. Equipment may be arranged parallel, at right angles, and at a variety of other angles.

Equipment Needed

A variety of large apparatuses are needed; they can be boxes, benches, bars, horses, hanging ropes, beams, or tables. Children should be in groups of 2 to 4 so that there is one station of equipment for each group of children. Mats should be placed beside and under equipment.

Description

"Today we are going to be doing balances on different pieces of equipment, and link our actions between the equipment. During this lesson it will be important to cooperate while sharing equipment.

"Before we do that, start by spreading out in the room for a warm-up. From a long sitting position stretch and touch your toes. Straddle your legs; lean right and touch

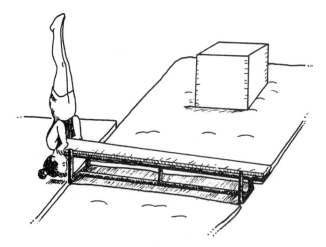

Figure 7.8   Equipment should be paired together.

your toes. Lean left and touch your toes. Twist around right and left to stretch your torso. Do a back bend. OK, stand up and do some other stretches.

"Begin running about—in and out, but do not touch the equipment. Good running steps, quick feet, high knees. Now when you get to a piece of equipment, travel over or along it, using your hands and feet. Move to open spaces and free equipment. I don't want to see long lines and children waiting a long time. Practice several ways of using your hands and feet on the equipment—maybe bunny-hops, walking, or cartwheel. [Signal stop.]

"This time, as you are on the equipment, stop and make a balance of your choice. The balance may be completely or just partially on the equipment. It may be upright or inverted. It may be symmetrical or asymmetrical. It may be a stretch, curl, or twist. As you come out of your balance, transfer your weight to the floor. You might use a jump or a roll. See what you can dream up. [Go and stop.] Now we have the beginning of a sequence. Run on the floor. Arrive at a piece of equipment. Travel on the equipment using hands and feet. Balance on the equipment. Move away. Start over. Try this again; make sure you visit all of the equipment as you travel about the gym. Use different balances at each of the pieces of equipment. Keep it going. [Signal stop.]

"Have you noticed that the equipment is arranged in pairs today? You might find a bench and box, bars and a bench, or a beam and box close to each other. Some are parallel to each other, others are perpendicular. You are to select one pair of apparatuses and develop a sequence there. The only rules are that there should be no more than four children at any one pair, and that you work cooperatively with the others at whatever place you choose. When it is not your turn, you should be watching and helping others by giving verbal suggestions, thinking of choices for your sequence, or practicing your sequence on the floor. Your sequence has to have these elements:

- At least one balance on each piece of equipment
- A traveling or rotation action to create a smooth transition between pieces of equipment
- A variety of body shapes, levels, inverted and upright, symmetrical and asymmetrical positions

"Experiment with some possible choices for 5 minutes. Select your best or favorite balances. Make the linking actions between balances smooth. For example, you could choose rolling, stepping, or wheeling actions to help you travel and transfer weight between pieces of equipment. You should not need extra steps to arrive at a piece of equipment. Feel free to move the equipment closer together or farther away or add an extra action to fill in the voids. The key is to make the flow natural—nothing extra, no glitches or hiccups. Practice until you get good at it. Then show your sequence to someone on the opposite side of the gym. [Signal go and stop.]

"After you've taken turns being a performer and an observer, talk to each other. Tell each other what you liked about the sequence. Give at least one suggestion on how the sequence could be improved. Go back and practice. Do the sequence again for each other. [When done] Did the sequence get better this time? How? [More polish, fewer glitches, better lines, better body stillness, eye focus.]

"Thanks for working so hard together today. I really like seeing you cooperate and help each other improve your work. It is exciting to see you become such good gymnasts and so responsible in your work habits. See you soon."

Look For

- Controlled, quality balances. Balances on the equipment and the floor must be held for 1 to 3 seconds. Whatever the balances, they should have good lines.

- Transitions, or linking actions, should be smooth and flow into and out of balance positions. No extra steps or wasted movements.

- Variety is important in the selection of balances—one high, one low; one symmetrical, one asymmetrical; one upright, one inverted. The children should make good choices.

How Can I Change This?

- Add complexity to the sequence by moving from the first piece of equipment to the second and back to the first, using three balances and two transition moves.
- Combine the balances on the two pieces of equipment with balances on the floor: balance on floor—transition—balance on equipment—transition—balance on floor—transition—balance on equipment—transition—balance on floor.
- Add a third piece of equipment. Balance on the three pieces of equipment with two transitions.
- Choreograph the sequence to a piece of music.

TEACHABLE MOMENTS

Observe a tape of some Olympic floor exercise, balance beam, or bar routines. Point out the balances and the smoothness of actions; one movement leads to the next. Explain that although the equipment and skill levels may differ, gymnasts at any level can strive for good balances and smooth transitions. Challenge them to be good gymnasts.

Have a discussion about what makes something interesting—whether in art, dance, or science. As a performer or as a spectator the answers usually involve competence and variety. The better individuals become at something, the more challenged and engrossed they feel to continue. Variety creates new challenges. A spectator appreciates differences and contrasts. Gymnasts seek variety in their balances and sequences to please themselves and spectators.

LEAN ON ME

Objectives

As a result of participating in this learning experience, children will improve their ability to

- select and demonstrate three or more partner-balances in good form, including good counter-tension and counterbalance
- link partner-balances with traveling and rotation skills to develop a sequence (5-6, #4)
- wisely select a partner (based on ability level, body size, and weight) with whom they can work productively (5-6, #27)

Suggested Grade Range

Intermediate (5–6)

Organization

A large open space is needed. Children should spread out in scatter formation, with a set of partners at each mat or padded area.

Equipment Needed

Mats and/or carpet squares are needed for this activity. Provide 1 mat or carpet square for every 2 children and 5-10 photocopies of Figure 7.9.

Description

"Today you will work with a partner to create balance shapes. In fact, you'll do the whole lesson with a partner. Choose someone who you know you can work productively with—not necessarily your best friend. You should consider size, weight, strength. Stand next to your partner now. Good. Let's start by playing follow-the-leader. The leader may choose to hop, skip, jump, cartwheel, or whatever. When you get to a mat, you may choose to roll. Don't go too fast, so that your partner can stay with you. Consider changes of direction, pathway, speed, the method of travel, the method of rotation, and the level. After a few minutes allow your partner to lead.

"Now go with your partner to a mat and sit down next to it. We'll work for a bit on strength and flexibility. First, stand facing your partner. One person put their arms straight out in front. Press your palms up, while your partner creates resistance by pushing down. Now press your arms out, while your partner provides resistance by pushing in. Next press your arms in, while your partner provides resistance by pushing out. Take turns with your partner.

"Stand with your back to your partner, arms raised to side and back. Have your partner gently and safely pull your hands closer together, arms parallel to floor. Finally stand back-to-back with your partner and hook elbows. One of you rocks forward and lifts the other onto your back. Feel your tummy and legs stretch?

"I am going to show you a few pictures of partners balancing. In any partner-balance the partners must use good principles of counter-tension and counterbalance to be successful. If one partner leans one way, the other partner must lean in the opposite direction to create a balance. Look at these pictures carefully and decide, together with your partner, on three balances which you would like to try. Go to your mat and try them. Feel free to come back and look at the pictures. You can also invent some partner-balances of your own. Be safe but see what you can do. Work until you can do three different balances. Be sure to choose balances that both you and your partner can do.

"A partnership requires both people working together. If one particular partner-balance doesn't work, change it so you can do it or try a different one. Notice that some balances take the partial weight of your partner. Others take your partner's complete weight. Select ones that you can do best. [Signal go and stop.]

"Now that you can do three different balances, let's think about how to get into and out of those balances smoothly. How do you get from here to there? For example, as the base, one partner could roll into a back-lying position from a forward, backward, or sideways direction. The second partner then could use a roll, cartwheel, or stepping action to arrive at the head, feet, or side of the support person. Once there, without hesitation move smoothly into the partner-balance. Go back and try each of your balances. Work hard at smooth transitions into, then out of your balances. Move to arrive—hold—move out. [Signal stop.]

"Finally, we'll build a sequence. Choose two of your three balances. Start your sequence with an individual balance away from your partner. Use some form of weight transfer to arrive. Go into your partner-balance. Move away to a second individual balance. Move together to your second partner-balance. Finish and hold. Your individual balances may mirror, match, and contrast shapes or levels. [Self-balance—move—partner-balance—move—self-balance—move—partner-balance.] Go to work. Do your best! If you need some help, come and ask. [Signal stop.]

"OK—several minutes have passed. I can see that you're working very hard. Wherever you are in developing your sequence, show it to a second pair and allow them to comment. Be constructive and helpful in your comments. What do you like? What suggestions for additions or improvements do you have? Go back and practice your sequence. Work hard for several more minutes to polish your routine. I want to see stillness in the balances, good timing, smooth transitions in your traveling or weight transfer actions.

"Stop. Everyone come in. You will now receive a gymnastics routine score sheet [see the appendix]. You are going to be asked to judge one new set of partners, whose routine you have not seen, using the rating scale I give you. Watch the routine twice. Rate it on quality for each of the elements on the scale. You will be looking for five elements worth 2 points each, or a total of 10 points. When you see errors deduct a half point. At the bottom of the score sheet be sure to write something you liked about the sequence. When you are finished, put your rating sheets in the box on my desk over in the corner of the gym. Thanks for your hard work."

Look For

- Children need to use good alignment and strong bases of support to take each other's weight (Figure 7.9). Good body mechanics are a must: knees over the feet, hips over the knees, and shoulders over the hands. The top person should place the weight in positions of strength, not in the middle of a sagging back.

- Children may need suggestions on how to create smooth transitions into and out of a balance. In general, the base person needs to arrive just ahead of the top person, to settle and be ready to assume the partner's weight. The top person must initiate an action to move away. Rolls, twists, turns, and stepping actions often create the best transitions.

- Some partners will go right to work. Other children will be more hesitant or begin by talking. Your job is to keep everyone task-oriented and productive. Give suggestions; pull back and observe. Make sure everyone makes enough practice attempts.

How Can I Change This?

- Simplify the sequence. Use one partner-balance with one self-balance before and after it.

- Add more complexity by using three–partner-balances with appropriate transitions into and out of each balance.

Figure 7.9   Sample partner balances.

- Focus on partner relationships. For example, all traveling actions and rotations could have a face-to-face or side-by-side orientation. One partner could move above and the other below.
- Focus on timing. Perform one of the weight transfer or rotation actions quickly and a second slowly, in a sustained fashion, to create contrast.

TEACHABLE MOMENTS

Emphasize good balance principles such as the base of support and center of gravity, keys to the success of partner-balances.

Bring in pictures that emphasize balance. Old cantilever structures, flying buttress structures, buildings by Frank Lloyd Wright and other architects, the work of Alexander Calder and other artists are examples.

Chapter 8

Learning Experiences for Rotation

This chapter includes eight learning experiences within the skill theme of rotation. LEs have been developed for the three categories of rotation: characteristics of rotation; principles of rotation; and movement around the vertical, horizontal, and transverse axes. The following outline provides a glance at the focus and suggested grade range of each learning experience.

Focus	Name	Suggested grade range
Rotation of the body: rocking, rolling	Balls, Eggs, and Pencils	Pre-K–2
Rotation of the body: rocking, rolling in backward direction	You've Got It All Backward	1–2
Principles of rotation: radius of rotation	Sit-Spins	2–3
Rotation of the body: rolling in a forward direction	Roll, Roll, Roll Your Body	3–4
Movement around the vertical axis: turns	Taking a Spin	3–4
Movement around the transverse axis: cartwheels	The String Challenge	3–4
Rotation of the body: using equipment	A Roll by Any Other Name . . .	3–4
Movement around the horizontal axis: around equipment	Hip Circles	5–6

BALLS, EGGS, AND PENCILS

Objectives

As a result of participating in this learning experience, children will improve their ability to

- demonstrate control in simple rocking and rolling actions
- select, from a variety of choices, ways to move into and out of a roll (K, #9)
- put a simple sequence together involving a travel, roll, balance (1-2, #17)

Suggested Grade Range

Primary (Pre-K–2)

Organization

A large open space is needed. Children should be in scatter formation with 1 or 2 to each mat or carpet square.

Equipment Needed

1 mat or carpet square for every student, or at least for every 2 students

Description

"Good morning! Today we will learn how to make our bodies roll, as a way of turning around. But, first, let's warm up. Our lesson is about turning, so let's start by jogging. As you jog, turn your body in a spinning fashion around a vertical axis, like a beater on a mixer, but not too fast. Stay under control. Be careful not to bump. Go easy, round and round. Can you hop on one foot and turn around? What about using two feet to jump and turn around?

"We don't want to do that too long or we'll get dizzy. Everyone, find a mat or carpet square and sit down beside it. We'll start our rolls as part of warm-up and stretching. Everyone get in our long sitting, or "gymnast-sit" position. Reach one hand way across your body. Keep your legs, bottom, and tummy tight as you roll over and return to a long sitting position. You just rolled, or transferred weight, from your seat, to your side, to the front, to the other side, and back to your seat. We'll call that a *seated-roll*. Easy.

"Try it again, rolling back in the other direction. Good! This time, roll halfway over into a push-up position. We call this a *front-support position*. Arch your back up like an angry cat. Now let your back sag and stick out your tummy like a happy cat. Nice! Roll the rest of the way and come back to your long sit.

"Now, tuck up into a ball—bring your knees and chin to your chest. Rock back and forth, from your back to your shoulders, and then to your feet. Rocking is like rolling—you transfer your weight from one body part to the next. It's kind of like a rocking chair. Try rocking back and forth. Think about how you're transferring your weight. Stay tucked in tight, like a ball, to help you. Now lie down and open up into a long stretch, just like a pencil. Keep your legs, bottom, and tummy tight and see if you can rock to one side and then the other. Rock from side to side. Keep it up. Yes! That's good. That's pretty easy, right? OK, stop.

"We are ready to roll now. A roll helps you turn over from one body part to the next. Adults call that *weight transfer* from one body part to the next. The secret to good rolling is to make yourself round in the direction you are moving. When I say "go," try rolling like a pencil. I want to see tight bodies. Choose one direction and roll from your back, to your side, to your front, and your side. Go. [During practice] Can you roll over and over three times? What about going the other direction to your other side? Keep in your personal space! Stop.

"This will be fun—you'll get to feel like a pretzel. Watch what I [or have a student demonstrate] do, and then you'll get to do it. First get into a kneeling position on your hands and knees. Pick up one hand and lead it through your body tunnel and out the hole between your other arm and leg. Lower your shoulder and begin rolling: shoulder—back—hips—feet—kneel. You want to keep your head off the floor. Try it now. [During practice] Stay tucked, like for a fall. Make it smooth—I don't want to hear your body hitting the floor. Now use the other hand to lead the other way, with the other arm through the tunnel. Try both ways by yourself a few more times. [Signal stop.]

"OK. Let's tuck up into an egg shape and roll sideways. Good, Karen and Joey, from your shins—side—back—side—shins. Roll the other way [direction] too. Try these in your own space a few times. [Stop.]

"This next one is a little harder. I'll have Jeremy and Shonda show you first. Squat down, hands on the floor just in front of you. Tuck your body—knees and chin close to your chest. OK, now raise your bottom, look under your legs, and let yourself roll! Try to keep your head off the floor. Are you ready to try it? Remember, tuck—behind up—roll! Try it in your space now. [During practice] Stay tucked. Your weight goes from feet to hands, to shoulders, to back, to hips, to your feet. Nice tuck, Johnny. Nice, keeping your head off the floor, Cindy. Try a few more rolls. Stop.

"We now know several ways to roll. Who remembers one way? Yes, Sheryl, seated. Good, we also have the [pencil, shoulder, sideways like an egg, and forward like a ball]. What I want you to do now is think about how to get into and out of these rolls. For example, can you go into a roll from standing? Sure. Let's get ready to try this. Lower your body into a squat, and then roll. Try this a few times. Nice tuck, Arisa! Stop. This time, choose a balance on three or four body parts and see if you can roll out of that balance. I'm going to come around and watch. Try different balances and go into different rolls—not just forward. Stop.

"You can end your roll in different ways. Let's see if you can figure some of these ways out. [If you see students do these, pinpoint them to other students. If not, suggest that students try each way.] *Straddle-seat*: Crouch on two feet using a knee and a foot with your body straight, two knees with your body straight. *V-seat*: Straddle on two feet. Practice several different ways now of finishing each roll—your choice [stop].

"Let's finish by putting a short sequence together. You'll travel on the floor, using good running, hopping, jumping, or skipping. When you come to a mat, lower your body, roll, get back up, and move a different way to the next mat. Try a different roll at each mat you come to. So it's travel—roll—and—travel again. Go! [Signal stop.]

"Everyone, come here quickly. Sit down. Who can tell me how to make your body roll really well? Yes, you must be round and stay tight, or tucked. When you rock or roll, where does your weight go? Right, from one body part to the next and to the next. What directions can we rock or roll? Good, Rinji—forward, backward, and sideways. What were the names we gave to the rolls today? Yes, Tonja, seated, pencil, shoulder, egg, and forward rolls. Good remembering! What shapes were our bodies in when we did all of these rolls? Yes, Felipe, long stretched [egg, ball, curled]. You sure learned a lot today. See you next time."

Look For

- In pencil or log rolling actions, children tend to initiate the action with the upper torso, so the legs trail. They should contract stomach, bottom, and leg muscles so the body rotates as one unit (see Figure 8.1).

- In forward rolling actions and the shoulder roll, children tend to open up, or become "unglued." This is a reflex action. They can grasp the shins to stay tucked: chin and knees to the chest (Figure 8.2).

Figure 8.1   A sideways pencil (log) roll.

Figure 8.2   When rolling forward, children should stay tucked in a ball.

Figure 8.3   A roll can be finished in various positions, including a straddle position or V-seat.

- To finish a roll in a different position or body shape, control must be established. It helps to perform the roll more slowly and to keep the muscles tight, rather than flopping and letting go (see Figure 8.3).
- Momentum is a key to any rocking or rolling action. The initial push or falling action should generate enough momentum for the body to make a complete roll without extra, unwanted movement. For example, in a forward roll the body should be round and tucked, and weight should return to two feet. No extra hand movements on the floor should be necessary to regain balance at the end.

How Can I Change This?

- Work on an individual sequence at one's own mat. Travel to the mat—lower—roll—resolve into a balance.
- Combine turning and spinning traveling actions with rolls on the mat. Approach with a spin, turn, or whirl. Then jump, land, crouch, and roll.
- Change the sequence. Roll out of one balance into a new balance. Balance—roll—balance.

TEACHABLE MOMENT

Bring several objects to class, such as a pencil, egg, ball, orange, cube, rectangle, and cone. Talk about the properties of things that roll smoothly: They are round, transfer weight from one place to next easily, and move around an axis. Why do some things not roll smoothly? They are flat and have edges or corners.

YOU'VE GOT IT ALL BACKWARD

Objectives

As a result of participating in this learning experience, children will improve their ability to

- demonstrate control in rocking and rolling actions in a backward direction
- select, from a variety of choices, ways to move into and out of rolling in a backward direction (1-2, #1)
- put a simple sequence together involving a travel, roll in a backward direction, and balance

Suggested Grade Range

Primary (1–2)

Organization

A large open space is needed. Children should be in scatter formation with 1 or 2 to each mat or carpet square.

Equipment Needed

1 mat or carpet square for every 1 to 2 students; blue and red poker chips and a box to put them in

Description

"Hi. Today is backward day. Everything we do is going to be backward. We'll start by running backward. Good running! Stay on the balls of your feet. Use quick feet. Be careful to watch where you're going. Move to open spaces. Who can jump backward? Try short, quick jumps. Now try longer jumps. What about hopping backward? When one foot gets tired, use the other. Can you skip or gallop backward? Try that! [Stop.]

"Move to a mat or carpet square. Watch me show you what to do next. You'll squat down into a ball shape, with your knees and chin to your chest. Stay up on the balls of your feet. Also stay tucked, but put your arms up and point your thumbs to your ears. From there, you'll rock back to your heels, then to the seat, to your back, your shoulders, your hands on the floor. Stay tucked up as you do it. Ready to do it on your own? Try it a few times. Each time, start all over from a squat [signal go and stop]. This time, when you go back, I want you to stay tucked up. See how Audrey is doing it? From there, push with your hands and rock back in the other direction: shoulders—backs—hips—feet. OK? Do this several times on your own. [During practice] Stay tightly tucked. [Signal stop.]

"You're doing great. Now we are going to try to roll *all* the way over backward. We are going to try it several different ways, from easy to hard. You choose the way that you think is best for you. [Have a student demonstrate the choices you present. Perhaps introduce three; invite students to try additional choices you may later present.]

- [*Entry level*] We all have this big thing on top of our shoulders called a head. It gets in the way of rolling backward. We are going to get in our backward-rocking squat. Tilt your head to one side and put your ear on your shoulder. You have now made a big open space to roll over, on the other side: tilt left, roll right. Ready? Crouch, feet, hips, back, shoulders, over to the feet.

- [*Backward roll on an inclined plane*] To create an inclined plane use a folded mat as a base to raise one end of two benches placed beside each other. Place a mat on top of the benches. (See Figure 8.4.)
- [*Backward roll on a level surface*] Squat, tuck, rock back, push with hands, back to feet.
- [*Backward roll from a stand*] Stand, squat, rock, push, feet.
- [*Backward roll into a straddle-stand*] Stand, squat, roll, straddle your legs.
- [*Backward roll from pike position*] Stand, pike, hands, rock back, push, extend, pike, stand.
- [*Backward roll from stand into extension*] Stand, squat, rock, push, extend (handstand position), snap down to feet.

[All children within a class should have practice with a backward roll that is appropriate for them.]

"Now that everyone can roll backward at least one way, we will work at selecting ways to move into and out of your rolls. It's like asking the question, "What's next?" or "Where do I go from here?" One choice is to use traveling actions on your feet. For example, you could run, jump, land, squat, roll, return to your feet, and move on. Another choice is to create a balance, roll backward, which is a weight transfer, out of that balance into a new balance or onto a knee and a foot, onto two knees, or onto two feet, and then move into another traveling action. For example, you could go from a shoulder stand, roll over backward to a knee and a foot, push up into a cartwheel, and travel off on your feet.

So let's summarize what kind of sequence you can create using a backward roll. You can

- travel, roll backward, travel;
- travel, roll backward, balance; or
- balance, roll backward, balance.

"While you work at your own mat or carpet square, I want you to try one or two of these ideas. Practice each one three or four times. Then choose the one sequence you like best, and work at it a few more times to get the bugs out. Go! [During practice] I want to see stillness in the balances, good lines, and good shapes. I want to see smooth backward rolling actions. And remember, work on smooth transitions into and out of balances and rolling actions. OK, stop. Now that most of you have your sequence memorized and in good shape, find a partner to show it to. Partners, tell the performer what you liked about their sequence. Maybe make one suggestion on how to change or improve it the next time. Then show them yours.

"Stop. Come in. Who can tell me what we worked hard on in today's lesson? Right, rolling backward. What were some ways we tried rolling backward? Good, you remembered. Inclined plane, from a stand, into a straddle stand. I am going to show you a backward roll. As you leave, if you think I do it well—with good form and all the right ways—put a blue poker chip in the box at the door. If you think my form could be improved, put a red poker chip in the box [see chapter 5 for the poker chip survey]."

Look For

- Rolling backward is difficult for young children until they learn to inhibit the postural reflex to open up. It is critical to help them learn to stay tucked, knees to the chest and feet close to the seat.
- Proper positioning of the arms and hands is critical: arms bent, elbows up, hands flat on the floor, thumbs in close to the ears (Figure 8.4). Each factor is critical to the success of getting enough lift to clear the head in a successful backward roll.
- Sufficient arm strength is critical to rolling in a backward direction. Before this lesson make sure you have the children take weight on the hands in a variety of ways to build arm strength.

Figure 8.4 Sample variations of the backward roll.

How Can I Change This?

- Add a bench or box. Use the backward rolling action to move toward or away from the equipment in the creation of a sequence.
- Work with a partner. Create a short partner sequence using a backward roll: Travel side by side, jump, land, roll, symmetrical and matched balance.

TEACHABLE MOMENT

Doing anything backward is unnatural. We do not have eyes in the back of the head; we cannot see where we are going. Sitting down in a chair, walking backward along a line, and walking backward on a balance beam will help develop tactile-kinesthetic perception. As children learn to use all their senses, they will develop better spatial awareness.

SIT-SPINS

Objectives

As a result of participating in this learning experience, children will improve their ability to

- spin around several times, under control, from a sitting position
- combine actions of spinning with balances, traveling, and weight transfer into simple sequences on the floor and on boxes or benches
- describe how lengthening and shortening the radius of rotation affects the rate of spin (3-4, #21)

Suggested Grade Range

Primary (2–3)

Organization

A large open space is needed. Boxes, benches and mats or carpet squares should be in scatter formation, spread out to permit free movement. One mat should be beside each piece of equipment.

Equipment Needed

1 mat or carpet square for each child, or at least every 2 children; 1 box or bench for every 2 children

Description

"We are going to have fun today learning how to make our bodies spin and rotate like a top! Let's begin first with light, soft running. Run at someone, and as you get close, avoid them. Approach big, fade, and move away. Relax—don't be stiff. This time do a high five with people you meet. You'll run, approach, jump, land, and then move away. [After several tries] Stop.

"Now, let's take that same idea of run—approach—jump—land to open spaces. This time you'll be working by yourself. Each time you run, you will hurdle or spring-jump into the air and rotate a quarter or half turn to face a new wall when you land. Use your head, feet and arms to help you spin, like this [demonstrate]. Notice how I moved my head and arms in the direction I was spinning? As you land, spread your arms and legs to help you balance. Bend and land under control. Ready? Go. [During practice] As you get better, you can go faster in your approach. As you take off, hurdle into the flight (one foot to two feet) like a diver or a vaulter. If you are really good, you might try rotating three-quarters or a full turn. Control is important. Stick your landings before moving on. Run, hurdle, jump, turn, land (squash), move on. [Signal stop.]

"Let's sit on the floor in a long sitting position. Get on the floor, rather than on a mat, right now because we need a slippery surface to do the next skill. Watch what I do first; then you'll try it. Tighten your tummy and your legs and get into a V-seat position. Swivel both legs to one side and place both hands on the floor on the other side. Push hard with the arms and swivel legs back to the other side. Do this several times so you build momentum [push, swivel, push, swivel, push, swivel]. Try this on your own. [Signal go and stop.] As you do it this time, push hard, then tuck your knees to your chest and grab your arms around your shins. Try this and see what happens. Yes, you spin round and round fast! If you shorten your body, you spin faster. Next time, at the end of your spin, lengthen your body back to the V-seat. Lengthening your body helps slow the spin. Try this several times. [During practice] Get control by spinning on your seat. We don't want any wipe-outs by spinning off onto backs or shoulders. Move your body parts symmetrically to help keep control. OK, stop.

"Let's see if we can put these sit-spins into a sequence on the floor. You'll run—hurdle—jump—land, just like before. Then lower—V-seat—sit-spin, then—resolve your sit-spin with a roll into a balance of your choice. Can you remember all that? Practice it several times so your sequence gets good. Go. [During practice] Work for quality. [After repeated practice signal stop.]

"Next, let's try doing sit-spins on the equipment. First, find a space on a box or bench. [Allow time] When you do your spins on the equipment, I want to see perfect control on your sit-spins. Go. [During practice] Good, I see nice, tight bodies. You look like gymnasts with good control. Try to spin faster once you feel comfortable on the equipment. Tuck your bodies during the spin to go faster. Try spinning in both directions. Stop. This time, use your hands and arms to control and finish your spin, and end with your whole body lengthwise on the bench [or box] with your back or shoulders supported on the bench. [Signal go and stop.]

"Next, do a sit-spin and freeze in a shape of your choice. Think, "Where can I go from here?" as you continue on the equipment or exit the bench or box onto the floor. Use different types of weight transfer such as rolls or a stepping action. Explore. Stop. I want to show you some of the ways your classmates have solved this challenge. [Pinpoint several students.] Some of your classmates linked their sit-spins with shoulder balances or a roll or a rocking action on the equipment. Some children ended their sit-spins in different positions, such as a V-seat, straight legs, or one leg straight and one leg bent on the bench. When the sit-spin ends with straight legs, you should take it into a full body roll onto the mat or a stepping action onto the feet. Try some of these ways and others that you can think of. Go. [During practice] You've got the idea. Work hard! I want to see controlled movements—no flops! [Signal stop.]

"You've done a great job with sit-spins both on the floor and on equipment. I want you to have a chance to create a movement sequence to demonstrate your talents. Your sequence should begin with a sit-spin on the equipment, move out of the sit-spin and off the equipment in any way you choose, then include a roll, and balance. Work for good quality. You are going to perform the sequences for your classroom teacher when he/she comes in to meet you. I want you to show him/her your best work. [Signal go and stop.]

[To the classroom teacher] "Welcome to the end of our class. Today we have worked very hard at developing a new skill called a sit-spin. Everyone has developed a sequence. First one half of the class will perform their sequences. Then the other half will do the same. We want you to notice all of the sit-spin actions and watch the variety of ways the children move out of the sit-spins into a roll and balance. [Performances.] Thank you for being our audience. The class is really working hard in gymnastics."

Look For

- Control in rotation. The use of the arms, legs, head, etc. is important in initiating and stopping rotation. Emphasize good control, including an aesthetic, focused, controlled sense of spin (see Figure 8.5). It feels good and is fun for youngsters. What you don't want is crash-and-burn, with students sprawled out all across the floor.

- Sit-spins on the bench must be controlled to prevent children from losing balance and falling off equipment (see Figure 8.6). Mats should be placed under the equipment. Children can help serve as spotters to provide safety.

- Transitions or linking actions in the sequence work. As children come to a stop from the sit-spin, their bodies should move quite naturally into a rocking, rolling (weight transfer), or balancing action. No holes, gaps, long breaks, or breakdowns should be evident.

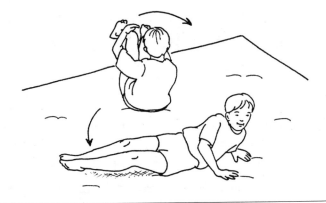

Figure 8.5 Children should do a controlled push, tuck, and spin.

Figure 8.6 Sit-spins can be performed on equipment.

How Can I Change This?

- Simplify the sequence if necessary: Start in a V-seat, sit-spin, transfer weight to a balance of the student's choice on the floor.

- Have students move into a sit-spin on the equipment and incorporate that into the sequence: mount—balance—sit-spin—balance—dismount.

> ### TEACHABLE MOMENTS
>
> Make sure children understand the principle of lengthening and shortening the radius of rotation. A shortened radius (body tuck) will cause a faster spin; a longer radius will make the spin slower and more controlled.
>
> Illustrate the use of this principle in other gymnastics skills (handsprings, somersaults) and such sports as diving, figure skating, dancing, and roller skating.
>
> Relate the rotary action to a spinning top or a bicycle wheel. What else do you know that is affected by shortening or lengthening the radius of rotation (swings on a playground, pendulum on a grandfather clock)?

ROLL, ROLL, ROLL YOUR BODY

Objectives

As a result of participating in this learning experience, children will improve their ability to

- demonstrate a variety of exits from a forward roll
- perform a forward roll from a stand, a forward roll in a pike position, and a forward roll in a straddle position
- develop a creative movement sequence that involves a combination of five rolls, with at least one of those rolls performed fast and a second roll slow (3-4, #26)

Suggested Grade Range

Intermediate (3–4)

Organization

Mats scattered around the room

Equipment Needed

1 mat or carpet square and 1 piece of chalk for each student

Description

"We will continue working with the concept of rotation today. To begin, find your own space on the floor. OK. Do some cartwheels in a circle [demonstrate]. You can either draw a big circle with chalk or imagine a big circle in your mind. [Signal go and stop.] Can you do cartwheels in a circle like a clock and then in the other direction [counterclockwise]? Make the cartwheels continuous. Try not to take any time between each cartwheel as you complete the circle. Try it again. Now, jog around the gym, and when you come to a mat, do a forward roll and then a cartwheel. You can do more than one forward roll on the mat if the mat is long enough. Go! [During practice] Land on two feet after you roll. Stay tucked throughout the roll. That's it! Freeze!

"Let's review some of the rolls we already know. From earlier lessons we know how to do seated rolls, forward rolls, pencil rolls, backward rolls, and shoulder rolls. Today we'll experiment with how these rolls can be resolved or finished. For example, when you start a regular forward roll, you can finish it in a long sitting position, on two knees, on a knee and a foot, on one foot, or coming to a stand on two feet. [Demonstrate one or a few of these options; see the lesson on shoulder stand in chapter 7.] You may have to twist or turn your body some as you rotate to finish in these positions. Try several different rolls and finish them in different ways. Go! [During practice] Pencil roll to V-seat. Backward shoulder roll to a knee and a foot. That's it; keep trying new ways. Good work! Stop.

"Everyone come and sit in front of this mat on the floor. I am going to show you how to do a roll from a standing position [demonstrate]. Stand tall. Take a walking step and begin to bend or lean forward. Lead with the opposite arm. As you lower your body, take weight on your forearm, then your upper arm, shoulder, and back. The idea is to use this as a safety roll if you think you are going to stumble and fall. Arm—shoulder—back—roll. Stay tucked throughout the roll and come up on your feet.

Sometimes you see volleyball players or martial arts performers roll like this. Any questions? Why don't you go to your space and try it? Try it many times. [During practice] Stay tucked in the roll. That's it. Try not to use your hands. Come up to a knee and a foot or return to a standing position on two feet. Stop.

"Sit down where you are and watch me. Next, we are going to learn how to do a roll in a pike position [demonstrate]. Start standing. Pike—hands—roll—*puuuush*—pike—stand. Place your hands on the mat and take your weight onto your upper back. Keep your head tucked. Your head and neck should never touch the mat. Go. [During practice] Instead of tucking your body as you have done in all the other rolls, keep your legs straight and your hips bent in a pike position. You can land in a long sitting position or try to come up to two feet. Coming up to two feet is a challenging task. Try it. [It may be better to teach only the skillful students this roll.] Stop.

"Finally, our last roll is a *straddle roll* [demonstrate]. Start in an erect standing position. Place your hands on the mat out in front of your body. Push with your legs. Tuck your head. Take your body weight on your upper back. Keep your legs straight and next sweep them wide to a straddle position. *Puuuush* your body up so you end up standing in a straddle position. Think stretch—hands—roll—straddle—*puuuush*! Try it. You have to roll quickly and really push your body up with your hands. If that is too difficult for you, end sitting on the mat in a straddled position. [Signal go and stop.]

"Your sequence for today involves a combination of five rolls of your choice. Who can tell me one of the rolls we have learned in this unit? Yes, Latasha, the shoulder roll [safety roll, backward roll]. OK, Mark, forward straddle roll [pencil roll, backward shoulder roll]. We have learned many different ways to roll. In your sequence the rolls must link smoothly together. Be sure I can tell when the sequence begins and when it ends. Be creative. One of the five rolls must be done fast and one must be done very slowly. Work hard on them. Show me how well you have learned to roll. Go!

"Stop. I want everyone to see the variety of roll sequences you have developed. Number off into three groups: 1, 2, 3 . . . OK. I want all 1s to show us their sequence while the 2s and 3s watch. Now it's the 2s' turn. Now it's the 3s' turn. To finish I am going to give you this 3 × 5 card and a pencil. On the card write down the names of three different rolls that you can do. Also write down three quick ideas that you think are important to help you roll well or smoothly. When you are finished, put your card in the box and line up. Thanks."

Look For

- Students having difficulty; be prepared to simplify the tasks. For example, allow for the legs to bend in the straddle roll. Remember, we want each child to be successful and to feel challenged at his or her own level.

- Rolling safely. Be sure students take their body weight on the upper part of the back and *never* on the head or neck.

- For doing a safety roll, the secret is achieving rounded body surfaces, transferring weight from one body part to the next, and giving with or lowering the body as it gradually moves from upright to rolling position on the floor (see Figure 8.7).

- Be sure students really *push* hard and extend upward with their arms on the pike and straddle roll (see Figure 8.8). It is very important for them to push with the hands to be successful.

How Can I Change This?

- For the more advanced children, these skills could be taught in an earlier lesson on rolling.

- After each new roll the students learn, have them link it to different actions, such as a balance, before you teach the next roll.

Figure 8.7   Forward safety roll.

Figure 8.8   Forward straddle roll.

- Add a piece of equipment. Use the rolls to approach the equipment or move away from the equipment. For less advanced children or children with less ability, allow them to finish their roll in a straddle/pike long sitting or a straddle/pike V-seat position. You could also allow them to bend their legs and press up into a standing position to finish the roll.

> **TEACHABLE MOMENT**
>
> Discuss the importance of rolling in various sports. Volleyball, baseball, football, and basketball, for example, have rolls for safety and for players to return to their feet quickly during play.

TAKING A SPIN

Objectives

As a result of participating in this learning experience, children will improve their ability to

- execute quarter, half, and full turns around the vertical axis during the flight phase of a jump
- land under control after rotating during the flight phase of a jump
- understand the roles of the head, arms, and legs in initiating rotation around an axis and in controlling the landing (3-4, #21)

Suggested Grade Range

Intermediate (3–4)

Organization

A large open space is needed for this activity, with mats, benches, and boxes spread out a safe distance. Mats should be placed beside a bench or box.

Equipment Needed

1 mat and bench or box for each student, 1 hula hoop or carpet square for each student

Description

"Today we will be jumping with turns in the air—like ice skaters! Let's start with good jumps. Everyone, use your feet in different ways to jump on the floor now. That's it: from two to two feet, from one foot to two, from two feet to one foot. Jump several quick jumps in a row, like hopscotch. Jump as high as you can. Let your jumps take you somewhere in the room. Travel forward, backward, sideways. Go straight, zigzag, in a curved line. [Signal stop.] Good.

"Now, each of you get a hoop [or carpet square]. Spread out and use the space wisely. Stand inside your hoop and face one wall. You'll try to jump and turn a quarter of the way around so you end up facing the next wall. Watch me [demonstrate]. As you do it, think about what you can do with your body to help you turn. Try it several times [signal start and stop]. OK. Who can tell me what body parts help to turn you? Yes, right, Billy, your arms move, or rotate, in the direction of the turn. Yes, Shelley, your head, too. Did you notice that your legs push in the opposite direction [action-reaction] to help you rotate? Let's see you use your arms, head, and legs [demonstrate] to get better turns now. Still quarter turns; think turn and land.

[After several tries] "Your turns are getting much better, but even with such good turns I still see some of you crashing to the floor on your landings. What can we do to land better? Yes, spread our feet apart, bend at the hips, keep our back straight, head up, and arms spread. Good. Now think spread, bend, and head up. Let's work at better landing now. Go. Yes, that's it, great!

[Move on to half and full turns with children who can handle the greater difficulty. Emphasize an increased use of the arms, legs, and head to initiate turns and control landings, as well as increased height to allow time to turn.]

"Now we will use turns to jump off the equipment. Place your hoop on the mat about one foot away from a bench or box. What you'll do is step up onto the bench [or box], jump down with a quarter turn, and land in the hoop. Think jump—turn—land—hold. Ready? Go ahead and try it. [After time for several tries signal stop.] Remember to land the same way you did when you were turning on the floor. Spread, bend, and head up! Count for 3 seconds to show control after you land. Try this now, thinking of landings. Stop. Now travel to all the different benches and boxes, and jump, turn, land, and hold at each one. [For those children who are doing well, allow half and full turns.] Stop.

"Go back to the piece of equipment where you started. Let's put the turns in the air into a sequence. Watch as I demonstrate. You'll start away from your bench or box, use your choice of steplike actions to approach the bench, jump up onto it with a one-foot takeoff, and two-foot landing. Then jump off, turn, and land. Go into a roll or wheeling action of your choice, and finish in a balance. The sequence is travel—jump—jump—turn—land—choice—balance. Work hard so you can show me your best. Go!

"Stop. I have seen some great sequences. You really have learned to make turns in the air during flight. Who can tell me what body parts help to get your turn going? Yes, the arms, head, and legs. How do you stop your turn when you land? Good—spread and bend. Very good, see you next time."

Look For

- Children who tend to jump out and land far away. The purpose of jumping with a vertical turn is to jump *up* to allow time for rotation and still get a controlled landing.

- *Head turn*—turn head in the direction of a rotation. *Wrap*—if gymnast is turning left, wrap the right arm around the body. *Push*—use the feet to push at takeoff, which will initiate the turning action from the floor (see Figure 8.9).

Figure 8.9 Children should jump and turn, landing softly.

How Can I Change This?

- Up to this point turns have been from a jump-forward orientation. Children could jump sideways or backward to initiate the turn. Have them start on the floor and, once control is established, do jumps off equipment.

- Try jumping with turns onto equipment. Start with quarter turns. As children gain confidence, allow them to do half turns.

TEACHABLE MOMENTS

Compare turns to the points of a compass: 90° equals a quarter turn, 180° equals a half turn, 360° equals a full turn.

Using the same style of orientation, use North, South, East, West.

Relate jumping and turning to simple science principles. Newton's Third Law of Motion—action and reaction—is used as the feet push down and away as the jump goes up and around. Wrap the arms to decrease the radius of rotation and turn fast. Spread the arms to slow down and stop, keeping the turn under control.

THE STRING CHALLENGE

Objectives

As a result of participating in this learning experience, children will improve their ability to

- transfer weight from the feet to the hands onto the floor, bench, or box and back to the feet as they rotate around the transverse axis (3-4, #4)
- develop strength in the arms and shoulder girdle (3-4, #16)
- develop flexibility in different joints by using stretching exercises

Suggested Grade Range

Intermediate (3–4)

Organization

A large open space is needed, with mats scattered around it. Place box or bench next to each mat.

Equipment Needed

1 piece of chalk, 1 long piece of string (6' to 8'), 1 box or bench, and 1 mat for each student; 1 photocopy of Figure 8.10

Description

"Today, let's begin by using different steplike actions from one mat to the next. When you come to a mat, take your weight on your hands and feet as you travel across it. Do bunny-hops along a bench or side-to-side, or even vault over the bench by putting your hands down and kicking your legs both to one side (*flank vault*). Remember to keep your arms straight and your bodies tight [signal start and stop].

"While we're still warming up, think of different ways to stretch your body. Stretching is very important to developing and maintaining flexibility in our joints. Try different stretches now to make sure you stretch the muscles in your arms, shoulders, back, tummy, and legs. Good. I see some back bends, Johnny is straddling his legs while sitting and bending forward; I see others, too. Think of four different stretches. Go over them several times and do each one well. [After a period of time] Team up with a partner now and teach your partner the four stretches—without talking. Then perform your partner's sequence of four stretches. Together choose the best four stretches from the eight stretches and put them into a sequence that you can do together.

"Now we are ready for the main part of our lesson, which is to take weight on the hands. As we take weight on our hands, we develop strength in the arms and shoulders. Gymnasts, and everybody else, too, need strong upper body muscles. Earlier you learned to take weight on both your hands at the same time. Today we are going to take weight on the hands one at a time. When I say go, everyone get a partner. You and your partner should get one piece of chalk and find a mat to sit down next to. You'll then draw this picture on your mat [show students Figure 8.10]. Go!

"Since I see you're all ready, we'll start by taking turns with your partner. You start on the letter *B* and stretch, topple, or fall forward, then lunge. If you are on the left B, place your left hand in the circle; then place your right hand on the other circle and come down on the right B, with one leg following the other. You land softly first on the leg you did not step with. Watch as Jeremy demonstrates. You want to think stretch—topple—lunge—hand—hand—foot—foot. Go ahead and try it; you get four

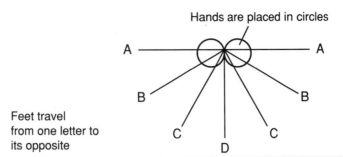

Figure 8.10 Diagram of a cartwheel performed over the string.

turns; then switch with your partner. The purpose of this is to develop upper body strength and the wheeling action of a cartwheel. The stretch—topple—lunge is a movement that helps make this a smooth sequence. Keep your legs and arms straight as you wheel around. Keep tight bodies; and land softly and in control. Go. [During practice] Try to do this from both sides of your body. Sometimes your right hand goes down first and sometimes your left hand goes down first. Stop.

"We are going to add a piece of string to make this a more challenging task. One partner, get a piece of string and tape and wait for my directions. [When all are ready] Tape the string down at the point where all the lines meet. One of you will hold the other end of the string up in the air for your partner. The string should be long enough so that whoever holds it can stand far enough away from the performer to avoid being kicked. The string can be held at various levels, depending on where your partner wants it. The higher the string, the more difficult the cartwheel is. If you are moving first, you place one hand on each side of the string, one at a time, and wheel your legs over it. Watch as I try it. I'm glad my string was low! Good quality is important—think of our stretch—topple—lunge—hand—hand—foot—foot. Go ahead and start, beginning and ending on the letter C. [Give other alternatives as necessary, using teaching-by-invitation or intratask variation.]

- Start on C, take weight on hands, return to the opposite C.
- Start on B, return to the opposite D.
- Start on B, return to the opposite C.
- Start on B, return to the opposite B.
- Start on B, return to the opposite A.
- Start on A, return to the opposite A.
- Tie or tape a piece of string to the top of a bench or box. One student holds up the string, and the other cartwheels from a position on the floor onto the bench or box, with the hands over the string and lands with the feet on the floor. The string should be long enough [6' to 8'] for the holder to stand far enough away from the performer to avoid being kicked.

[Signal stop.] "As you get better and feel more confident, have your partner raise the level of the string to increase the level of challenge. Make sure you try cartwheels over the string from both the left and right sides of your body. [More advanced students can learn advanced Olympic gymnastics skills of rotation through transverse and horizontal axes, such as front and back walkovers, roundoffs, and front and back handsprings as well. These are, however, beyond the scope of this book; please consult such references as Hacker et al. (1993) and Cooper and Trnka (1989).]

"Let's end our lesson with a movement sequence. Let's take weight on the hands, using a wheeling action. Perform a roll of your choice, then finish in a balance [wheel—roll—balance]. Practice this over and over until you are ready to perform it. Go! [During practice] Make sure you have good linking actions. One action should lead right into the next without stops or extra movements. Your sequence should flow together. Work hard. Are you ready to perform your sequence? Stop.

"Girls stand, boys sit. Girls, you will go first. Show us your sequence. OK, boys, it is your turn. Thanks! Everyone sit down. You're really learning a lot about cartwheels and rotation. Who can tell me what it takes to do a good cartwheel? Yes, Li, hand—hand—foot—foot. Straight arms and legs like spokes in a wheel. As I watched your sequence work, I saw many good efforts at smooth linking actions. I saw very few extra movements, stops, stutters, or glitches. Thanks for your hard work."

Look For

- Students keeping their arms and legs straight. Are their bodies tight, and their shoulders over their hands? Are they landing on the foot opposite the one they stepped with?

How Can I Change This?

- Do a sequence of: wheeling action—roll—balance—on the floor, with equipment, or with partners.
- Add a balance at the beginning: balance—wheeling action—roll—balance.

TEACHABLE MOMENT

Doing a cartwheel should be like a wheel turning on a bicycle. Your hands and feet are the tires. Your arms and legs are like spokes in the wheel. In order for the wheel to work well, the spokes need to be straight, tight, and stretched.

A ROLL BY ANY OTHER NAME . . .

Objectives

As a result of participating in this learning experience, children will improve their ability to

- demonstrate control in rolling actions used to move onto, along, or off equipment
- develop an action sequence that includes the use of a roll onto, along, or off equipment (3-4, #26)

Suggested Grade Range

Intermediate (3–4)

Organization

A large open space is needed. Children should be in scatter formation with 1 or 2 to each piece of equipment.

Equipment Needed

At least 1 box, bench, low beam, or table is needed for every 2 students. Folded mats 4" to 6" high can substitute. Mats and carpet squares should also be placed beneath or beside the equipment.

Description

"You already are very good at rolling in different ways and in different directions. Today we'll use rolls to move onto, along or off the equipment. It will be challenging for you! First, let's warm up by jogging on the floor in open spaces. Light, up on the balls of your feet with springy, quick feet. Change your speed, faster and slower. Change directions. Jog and, as you come close to a mat, transfer smoothly into jumps. As you get to the mat, go into a roll and return to your feet. Keep moving to another mat. Jog, jump, jump, jump, land, roll. Good! Stop!

"We'll start today by rolling *off* our equipment. Everyone, move to a piece of equipment you'd like begin at and sit down beside it. First we will get on our equipment in a squat or kneeling position. Watch as I do it first [or have a student demonstrate]. From this position place your hands down on the floor. Stay tucked, chin and knees to the chest. Rock forward a little and transfer your weight to your hands and arms. Make your arms strong. Your bottom goes up; roll over to your feet. Think you can try it? Go ahead, everyone try it a few times. Stop.

"What about rolling off sideways from a pencil position? Place one arm and leg down on the floor and roll. See if you can lie on your back or be in a shoulder stand and roll off backward. Use your hands to control your body position by holding onto the equipment. Go ahead and practice rolling off.

[Signal stop.] "Well, I see we can roll off! Now let's try rolling onto the equipment. Stand facing your piece of equipment, just like Danny and Meghan here. Put your hands on the equipment. Tuck your chin to your chest. Begin to lower your body and take your weight on your hands and arms. Jump, bottom up, tuck, and roll. Your weight should go from the feet, to the hands, to the shoulders, back, hips, and feet. Stay tucked [demonstrate]. Everyone try this. If you need to change to a different piece of equipment, you may—but ask the person who is there already. Good. Practice this several times. Stop.

"Next, you'll turn around with your back to the equipment. Sit on the equipment and rock back. Feel for the equipment with both hands beside your head. Stay tucked and push with your hands. Roll over to your feet [demonstrate]. This is a hard skill. Everyone may not want to do it. Some of you may want to do it with a spotter. See if you can find a way to roll onto the equipment in a sideways direction. [After a few minutes] Stop.

"In order to roll along a piece of equipment, it must be fairly long. We can use the tables, benches, and folded mats for that. [Surfaces should be wide and low to build confidence. Only accomplished children will want to use a 4"-balance beam.] Remember to try to do your rolls just as if you are on the floor. I will be looking for these pinpoints to make sure you are doing the skill correctly:

- Forward roll—tuck chin to the chest, bottom up, transfer weight to the hands, shoulders, back, hips, and feet
- Backward roll—tuck, weight goes from the feet to the hips, back, shoulders; push with the hands and back to feet
- Sideways roll—tight body, roll like a pencil or log

Try not to get nervous just because you are on an elevated surface. If you can do your roll on the floor on a line, with practice you will develop the precision and control on the equipment. We have started on low, wide surfaces on purpose for your safety. You can also ask for someone to help spot for you. [Mats can be stacked on both sides of a low bench or beam to reduce falling.] Practice each skill several times. Stop.

"Now let's put these rolls into a sequence. You may choose the type of sequence you want.

- Start with steplike travel to equipment, then a roll of your choice onto the equipment, finish in a balance on the equipment.
- Start in a balance of your choice on the equipment, roll off the equipment, finish in a balance of your choice.
- Start in a balance on the equipment, go to a roll of your choice along the equipment, finish in a balance of your choice on the equipment.

"Stop. Wow! I'm impressed, seeing the great variety as you perform your rolls onto, off of, and along the equipment. Let's show off your work. Everyone whose sequence involves a roll onto the equipment will perform their routine first. Everyone else, watch. Great ideas! Nice transitions! Now, everyone whose sequence involves a roll *along* the equipment, perform your routines. Yes, those were good quality rolls, and you maintained control. Finally, everyone whose sequence involves a roll *off* the equipment, perform your routines. I'm just as impressed with your work. Good weight transfers in your rolls off the equipment. They were smooth: I didn't see clunking or crashing. Thanks for your hard work."

Look For

- Children should execute these rolls on and off equipment as if they were on the floor (Figures 8.11 and 8.12). Good form and smooth weight transfer are keys.
- Some children may be very apprehensive about trying one or more of these rolls. Don't force the issue. Find their comfort level; simplify a given roll by stacking extra mats. Provide spotting for those who want it. Allow children to choose a roll they are comfortable with. First master the roll on a line on the floor.
- When sequence work starts, look for smooth transitions into and out of rolls, onto and off of the equipment, without extra steps, indecision, or glitches; with good control.

How Can I Change This?

- Make the sequence more complex by combining rolls. For example, steplike travel to equipment, roll onto equipment, balance on equipment, roll off equipment, finishing it in a balance.

Figure 8.11 Rolling off the equipment.

Figure 8.12 Rolling onto the equipment.

- Make up a partner-rolling sequence in which partners mirror or match each other. For example, use a cartwheel to arrive, jump onto equipment, lower into a balance of choice, roll off equipment, and finish in a balance of choice.

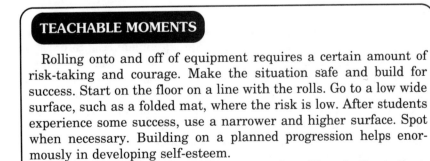

TEACHABLE MOMENTS

Rolling onto and off of equipment requires a certain amount of risk-taking and courage. Make the situation safe and build for success. Start on the floor on a line with the rolls. Go to a low wide surface, such as a folded mat, where the risk is low. After students experience some success, use a narrower and higher surface. Spot when necessary. Building on a planned progression helps enormously in developing self-esteem.

Teach for transfer. Make the conditions for rolling similar to those on the floor, using the same cues.

HIP CIRCLES

Objectives

As a result of participating in this learning experience, children will improve their ability to

- demonstrate controlled front and back hip circles on a large piece of equipment (5-6, #15)
- understand the principle of rotation around a piece of equipment
- perform a movement sequence that includes at least one front or back hip circle

Suggested Grade Range

Intermediate (5–6)

Organization

Equipment should be set up at an appropriate height such that students can safely spin around it. A bar set too high might prevent success for the less-skilled children. Bars or beams should be set at chest height for standing positions; children should be able to just reach the bar or beam from a long sitting position under the equipment. Spread mats under and around the equipment. Spread the stations around the gym.

Equipment Needed

A variety of large apparatuses must be available to conduct this lesson, including balance beams, parallel bars, and horizontal bars. If you have only 1 or 2 pieces of equipment, use them as stations and have the children rotate to the equipment. Ideally, you want enough large pieces of equipment to fit 4 to 6 students safely at each apparatus. For safety purposes there should be an adequate number of mats around the equipment. If you have sufficient mats, extend them out away from the equipment so that students can develop sequences moving toward or away from the equipment. 1 drum is necessary and outdoor playground pieces, such as chin-up bars, are also useful.

Description

"Today, we will use the idea of rotation in a new way with equipment. We are going to rotate around a beam or bar. This activity takes some abdominal, upper body, and arm strength, which we have been building up progressively during the year. Let's get started. To begin, jog around the room in any way you choose. Whenever I beat the drum, change the speed of the jog. Stay off the mats. Freeze! Get with a partner. Think of three stretches for your arms, trunk, and legs. Teach your partner the three stretches. You should do six different stretches altogether. Find a new partner and do the same.

"OK. When I say go, find a piece of equipment and stand in front of it, facing me. No more than four to six of you for each piece of equipment. Go! Support your weight on the equipment in a front-support position; it looks like this [demonstrate]. Take turns with a partner if the space is crowded. Your body and arms must be tight and straight. Your hips rest on the equipment. Keep your head up. Go!

[During practice] "Good. Hold it for 5 seconds. Try to hold it longer. Count to yourself: How long can you hold it? Your hands should be in a palm-down position, with the fingers away from your body (overgrasp) and shoulder-width apart. Great, I see strong, tight bodies with good lines. I even see toes pointed. Stop. Now, face the equipment; support your body weight on it and then lift one leg in a straddle position on it. Keep your legs straight and your head up. Keep your arms straight and tight, your shoulders over your hands. Come down to the front-support position. Now straddle your other leg on the beam. Swing, lean, straddle, and support. Give your partner a chance.

"What other balances can you create from a front-support position? How about swinging both legs to one side and balancing on one hand and your feet [one-hand releases]? How about straddling both legs simultaneously? You and your partner have a few minutes to practice different supports and balances. [Signal stop.]

"Next, we are going to do a form of front and back hip circles. We'll start with a front hip circle, which ends in a long sitting position under the equipment. Watch now [demonstrate, teacher or student]. Bring yourself into a front-support position. Grip the equipment with your fingers pointing toward you, thumbs away. Bring your body into a tuck position as you spin around the beam. End the rotation by sitting on the floor in a long sitting position [demonstrate]. Think support—tuck—spin—sit. Do this with control—no crashes to the mat. Go! [During practice] Keep your bodies tight. This will give you control. *Squeeze* your bottom and your legs. Stop. If you can do this well, I challenge you to do it with your legs straight, from a pike position. This takes more strength: Support—pike—spin—sit. Do it slowly and end up in a long sitting position on the mat under the beam (bar), just as Dawn did [demonstrate]. Try it. Good, I see slow controlled rotations around the beam (bar), with tight bottoms and legs. Keep your arms bent, so your body rotates closely around the beam (bar): This gives you better control. Once you sit on the mat, add an action away from it, such as a roll, a wave, or a twist back onto the beam (bar). Explore different ways [pinpoint a few students for demonstrations]. In a few minutes, I'll have some people show everyone what they've done.

"OK. Next you'll try a type of backward hip circle. This is another challenging task. You'll start in a long sitting position under the equipment with hands gripping it in an undergrasp, palms facing away from you. Pull up with your arms, to get the beam (bar) close to your chest, and kick one leg up and over the top of the beam (bar). Kick hard to get the momentum you need to get over the beam (bar). *Pull* and *kick*. End in a front-support position. Neat, huh? Give it a try. [During practice] Keep trying. This takes some strength and timing. You need to keep the equipment close to your hips to be successful. Have a controlled flowing action. Spotters can help you by supporting the kicked leg over the beam (bar). I want everyone to try this several times. Good work.

[More advanced students can learn Olympic gymnastics forward and backward hip circles as well: Please consult such references as Hacker et al. (1993) and Cooper and Trnka (1989).]

"For today's sequence, start with either a front or a back hip circle, move away from the equipment in a rolling action, taking weight on your hands, and end in a balance: Hip circle—rolling—weight on hands—balance. Remember to make smooth transitions from one action to another. Work for quality. I'm going to come around and watch you. Perform your sequence for a partner, also. Excellent work! That's it for today."

Look For

- When children are in a front-support position on the equipment, their arms should be straight, with shoulders over the hands. Bodies should be tight, legs straight, and toes pointed (see Figure 8.13).

- Proper grips must be used for the hip circles. Thumbs should always be in the direction of the turn. If the students' hands are small, they may have to change their hand position during the rotation to have a safe grasp. Teach this, watching closely: It is important for safety.

- Overweight children may lack the necessary strength for hip circles. Be on the alert for students who might not succeed and provide them with activities to improve their upper body strength.

- Make sure all rotation takes place with the body's center of gravity close to the bar or beam (Figure 8.14). It is much more efficient mechanically.

Figure 8.13 Sample balances from a front support.

Front hip circle

Back hip circle

Figure 8.14 Hip circles.

How Can I Change This?

- Divide students into small groups. Each group goes to a differently designed work station. At each station place a task card that gives students some guidelines for developing a creative movement sequence. For example, "Mount, balance, front support, hip circle, long sit, shoulder stand, roll, balance."
- Have students work with a partner and develop a short sequence that includes a hip circle. They can mirror or match each other's movements.

TEACHABLE MOMENTS

Teach the students what a good body line is in a front support on the beam. Take a broomstick or ruler and place it against the beam; explain how the child's body should look as straight as the broomstick or ruler.

Rotation around a bar or beam provides an excellent opportunity to talk about centrifugal and centripetal forces.

Forms and Handouts

As a teacher you may find this series of forms helpful for promoting and developing your gymnastics program. It begins with a gymnastics report card, which might be sent home with a child's academic report card. When using the report card a simple asterisk (*) can denote the skills a child has learned during the grading unit. Space at the bottom of the card allows teachers to write short comments about routines, or sequence work, and cognitive and affective assessment.

Next is a series of task cards as examples to use with individual or station work in a gymnastics setting. A series of balance puzzles, a gymnastics notation system, and a learning center sheet contain additional ideas for promoting individual and station work in gymnastics.

A sample award certificate for children's work in gymnastics and an individual and partner sequence are items to encourage the development of quality routines. Teachers, parents, older students, or peers can learn to use the subjective rating scale provided, much as regular gymnastics is judged. As long as they challenge themselves within their own levels of ability, less-skilled students can achieve high scores, just as the high-skilled students can, all of them receiving recognition for effort.

Gymnastics Report Card

Name _____　School _____

Teacher _____　Grade _____

Unit Work/Skills Mastered

Traveling

Steplike—using feet

- ❑ Walk
- ❑ Run
- ❑ Hop
- ❑ Jump
- ❑ Skip
- ❑ Gallop
- ❑ Slide
- ❑ Other locomotion

Steplike—using hands, feet, and knees

- ❑ Crawl
- ❑ Bear walk
- ❑ Crab walk
- ❑ Bunny-hop
- ❑ Mule kick
- ❑ Coffee grinder
- ❑ Walkover—front, back
- ❑ Wheeling
- ❑ Springing

Weight transfer

- ❑ Rocking, rolling
- ❑ Twisting, turning
- ❑ Sliding
- ❑ Tumbling

Flight

- ❑ Takeoff
- ❑ Suspension
- ❑ Landing
- ❑ Trampette work
- ❑ Vaulting

Statics

Characteristics of balance

- ❑ Moments of stillness
- ❑ Tightness of body
- ❑ Controlled

Principles of balance

- ❑ Base of support
- ❑ Center of gravity
- ❑ Balance, counterbalance
- ❑ Linking actions
- ❑ Movement into and out of balance

Types of balance

- ❑ Upright, inverted
- ❑ Symmetrical, asymmetrical
- ❑ Hangs
- ❑ Supports
- ❑ Relationship to equipment
- ❑ Individual, partner

Rotation

Principles of rotation

- ❑ Radius of rotation
- ❑ Eye focus

Movement around three axes

- ❑ Vertical
- ❑ Horizontal
- ❑ Transverse

Rotation of the body

- ❑ In space
- ❑ Around equipment

Routine/sequence work: components of sequence _____

_____

Knowledge assessment: _____

_____

Attitude/values assessment: _____

_____

Note. *indicates work during this grading period.

Examples of station task cards
that link themes in educational gymnastics

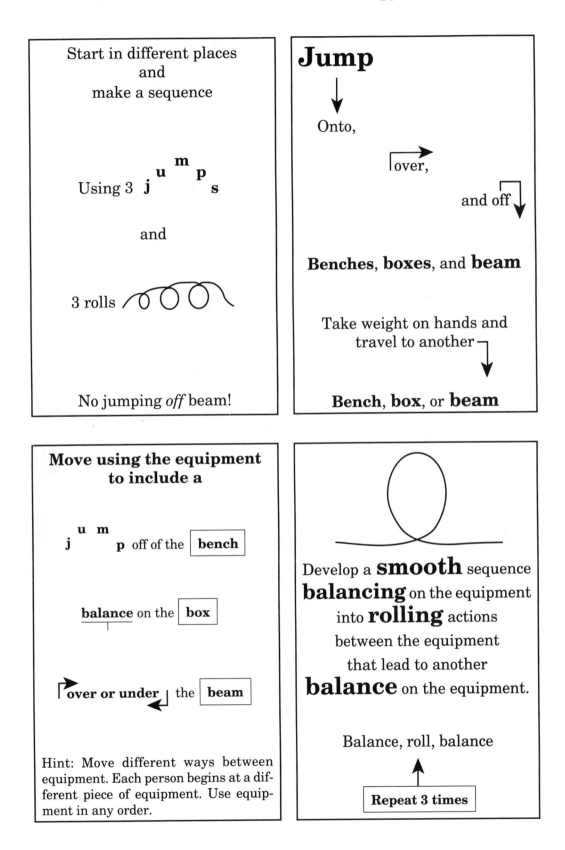

Start in different places
and
make a sequence

Using 3 j u m p s

and

3 rolls

No jumping *off* beam!

Jump

Onto,

over,

and off

Benches, boxes, and **beam**

Take weight on hands and
travel to another

Bench, box, or **beam**

**Move using the equipment
to include a**

j u m p off of the | bench |

balance on the | box |

over or under the | beam |

Hint: Move different ways between
equipment. Each person begins at a different piece of equipment. Use equipment in any order.

Develop a **smooth** sequence
balancing on the equipment
into **rolling** actions
between the equipment
that lead to another
balance on the equipment.

Balance, roll, balance

| **Repeat 3 times** |

Balance Puzzles

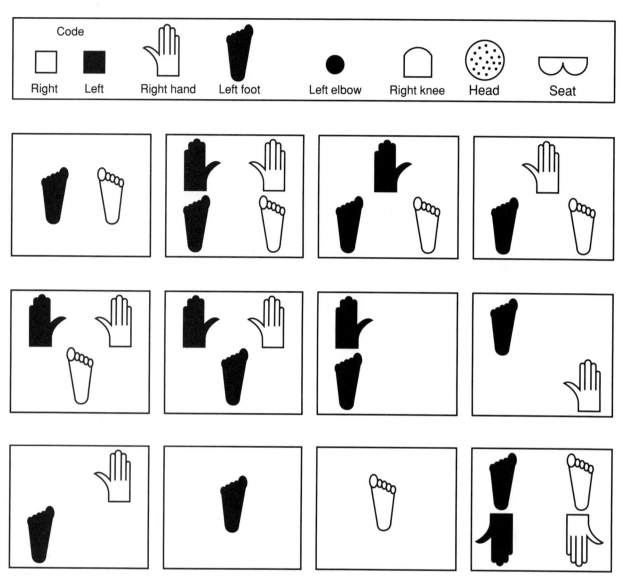

Balance Puzzles

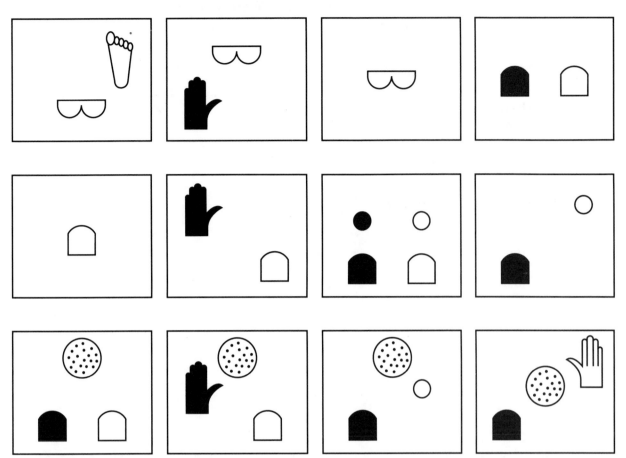

From *Perceptual Motor Development* (Vol. 1) (pp.13-14) by P. Werner and L. Rini, 1976, New York: Wiley.
Copyright © 1976 by Wiley. Reprinted by permission of John Wiley & Sons, Inc.

Write Your Sequence Using Gymnastics Notation
Gymnastics symbols for movements and concepts

Traveling actions

Feet: Walk – – –
　　 Run ᴡᴡᴡ
　　 Leap ⌒
　　 Jump ∧
　　 Hop ‖‖
　　 Skip ⊥
　　 Slide ▷

Weight transfer and rotation

　　 Cartwheel x
　　 Roundoff ͟x
　　 Bunny-hop ∧
　　 Walkover ʯ
　　 Roll ᴔ

Balance

　　 Hang ⊤
　　 Swing ⊔
　　 Support ⊤
　　 Backbend ⌒
　　 Headstand ⊔⊔
　　 Handstand ⊤⊤

Concepts

Direction

Up ↑
Down ↓
Forward →
Backward ←
Sideways ↔

Pathway

Straight —
Curved ∿
Zigzag ⇄

Relationship

Over ⤾
Under ⤿
Around ⟲

Level

Low ⊔
Medium ⊟
High ⊓

Speed

Fast ⟍
Slow •••

Symmetry

Symmetrical △
Asymmetrical ⋉

Invent your own symbols: ＿＿＿ ₃• = 3 times ＿＿＿＿＿＿＿＿＿＿＿＿＿＿

＿＿＿＿＿＿＿＿＿＿ ɪ = inverted ＿＿＿＿＿＿＿＿＿＿＿＿＿＿

＿＿＿＿＿＿＿＿＿＿＿＿＿＿＿＿＿＿＿＿＿＿＿＿＿＿＿＿＿＿＿＿＿

＿＿＿＿＿＿＿＿＿＿＿＿＿＿＿＿＿＿＿＿＿＿＿＿＿＿＿＿＿＿＿＿＿

＿＿＿＿＿＿＿＿＿＿＿＿＿＿＿＿＿＿＿＿＿＿＿＿＿＿＿＿＿＿＿＿＿

＿＿＿＿＿＿＿＿＿＿＿＿＿＿＿＿＿＿＿＿＿＿＿＿＿＿＿＿＿＿＿＿＿

＿＿＿＿＿＿＿＿＿＿＿＿＿＿＿＿＿＿＿＿＿＿＿＿＿＿＿＿＿＿＿＿＿

＿＿＿＿＿＿＿＿＿＿＿＿＿＿＿＿＿＿＿＿＿＿＿＿＿＿＿＿＿＿＿＿＿

Sample sequence: ＿＿＿＿＿ ‖‖3• ＿＿＿＿＿　Hop forward 3 times

　　　　　　＿＿＿＿＿ ᴔ ＿＿＿＿＿　Roll backward

　　　　　　＿＿＿＿＿ ⋉ɪ ＿＿＿＿＿　Asymmetrical balance, inverted

Your sequence:　　　　　　　　　1. ＿＿＿＿＿＿＿＿＿

　　　　　　　　　　　　　　　2. ＿＿＿＿＿＿＿＿＿

　　　　　　　　　　　　　　　3. ＿＿＿＿＿＿＿＿＿

　　　　　　　　　　　　　　　4. ＿＿＿＿＿＿＿＿＿

　　　　　　　　　　　　　　　5. ＿＿＿＿＿＿＿＿＿

Note. Original ideas presented by Stephen W. Sanders, J.T. Walker School, Marietta, Georgia, at the Southern District AAHPERD Conference, Nashville, Tennessee, February, 1980. Printed by permission.

Learning Center: Designing a Sequence

Objective:

When you have completed these activities, you will be able to perform a gymnastics sequence on the equipment provided.

Equipment:

This learning center can be performed on any of the pieces of equipment in the gym, such as a box, bench, beam, bar, or table.

What to do:

1. After choosing a piece of equipment, try several different ways of getting on or *mounting* safely. Try different ways of jumping, hopping, using hands and feet, or even a rolling or wheeling action. Use a forward, backward, or sideways direction.

2. Choose the mount you like best, then *balance* in a symmetrical body shape on two, three, or four body parts. Count to three while you hold your balance.

3. *Change* your balance to an asymmetrical balance using different body parts.

4. Find a way to get off or *dismount* your equipment safely.

5. Practice the whole sequence: Mount, balance, change, dismount. Do it several times, until it is easy. Then go to number 6.

Check for quality:

6. Is your sequence smooth with good linking actions? Are there extra steps, pauses, or hesitations?

7. Check your balance shapes for stillness and control.

8. Are you challenging yourself? If part of your sequence is too easy, change that part to make it more difficult.

How can I change my sequence?

9. Change the balance shapes—stretch, curl, twist.

10. Change the level of the balances.

11. Change the place you get on and off the equipment (end, side?).

12. Vary the speed during the sequence—start slowly and end quickly or start quickly and end slowly.

13. As you dismount the equipment, finish the sequence by adding a roll and a new balance on the floor.

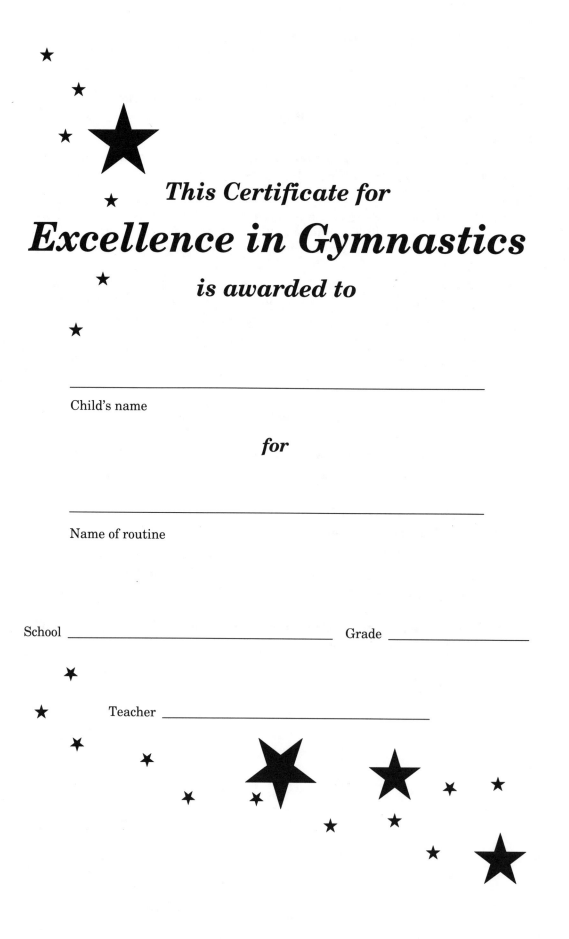

This Certificate for

Excellence in Gymnastics

is awarded to

_____

Child's name

for

_____

Name of routine

School _____ Grade _____

Teacher _____

Gymnastics Routine

Individual Sequence Using Bench or Box and Mats

Develop a floor exercise sequence on the bench and mats that includes the following components.

- A minimum of five balances will be included in the total routine.
- The sequence is to begin and end in a balance position.
- Balances should show changes of shape, symmetry and asymmetry, changes of bases and the number of bases of support.
- One balance must be inverted.
- One balance must include taking weight completely or partially on the bench or box.
- One traveling action must be steplike.
- One traveling action must involve taking weight on the hands.
- Other traveling actions may include rocking, rolling, and sliding.

Other considerations in the routine should include

- changes in the use of air and floor pathways,
- changes in speed (time),
- changes in level, and
- the use of relationships (from one body part to another; to the equipment as you approach or move away from it; or to the bench as you move on, over, or off of it).

Be aware of linking actions from one balance to another. What works smoothly to take you from one position to another? Be aware of line and technique in your work. Are your stretched shapes extended? Are your curved shapes rounded and smooth? Have you eliminated any unneeded actions?

You will be graded on these factors:
Balancing actions—2 points
Traveling actions—2 points
Use of the bench/box—2 points
Linking actions, transitions—2 points
Variety, aesthetic appeal—2 points

Gymnastics Routine

Partner-Balances With Mat

Develop a sequence with your partner on the mat that includes the following components.

- Routine will include three partner-balances.
- At least one of the three partner-balances will include one person taking the complete weight of the second person.
- The remaining two balances may include partially taking your partner's weight through balance and counterbalance.
- The beginning and end of the routine must include individual balances that show symmetrical, asymmetrical, mirroring, and matching balances; weight transfers into and out of the partner-balances; and traveling actions toward or away from one's partner.
- Use of levels, changes in body part relationships, body shape, directional changes, awareness of time will be included.
- A piece of music will be selected to accompany the routine. Choose music to emphasize smooth, flowing changes; quick changes; slow sustained changes in traveling actions, weight transfer, or balance positions.

Other considerations in the routine should include

- changes in the use of air and floor pathways, and
- changes in level.

Be aware of linking actions from one balance to another. What works smoothly to take you from one position to another? Be aware of line and technique in your work. Are your stretched shapes extended? Are your curved shapes rounded and smooth? Have you eliminated any unneeded actions?

> You will be graded on these factors:
> Choice of music—2 points
> Partner-balances—2 points
> Individual balances—2 points
> Traveling, weight transfer actions—2 points
> Aesthetic impression, transitions, flow—2 points

So Where Do We Go From Here?

We hope that reading this book has left you full of thoughts, some questions, and most of all, *excitement* about teaching this content area. We hope it makes you eager to get out there and try some of the ideas and learning experiences with your children . . . to take another closer look at your curriculum . . . to maybe give you that "something extra" you needed in order to take a second try at teaching this content to your children.

And although we know that implementing many of the ideas in this book with your children probably won't be quite as easy as it was to read about them, we hope that this book goes a long way in helping you to get there. We hope that it encourages you to talk with other teachers, ask questions, and search for solutions that will make your teaching, and your students' learning experiences, the best they can be!

We here in the Child Health Division of Human Kinetics want you to know that you're not out there alone in your quest to improve your teaching and the physical education experiences of your students. We do our best to provide you with current information and professional support through our many programs and resources. Examples of these include our American Master Teacher Program for Children's Physical Education (AMTP), which this book is a part of; the national newsletter *Teaching Elementary Physical Education (TEPE)*; the annual national Conference on Teaching Elementary Physical Education, which we cosponsor, and our outcomes-based student and teacher resources.

Many of you have written or called us in the past with a neat idea you wanted to share with others in *TEPE*, a question on where to find some information, or even just to say thanks for a job well done. We hope that you'll continue to let us know what your questions, concerns, and thoughts are and how we can help you even better in the future. Feel free to write us at P.O. Box 5076, Champaign, IL 61825-5076, or call us at 1-800-747-4457. We'll do our best to help you out!

Until then,

The staff of the Child Health Division of Human Kinetics

References

Belka, D. (1994). *Teaching children games: Becoming a master teacher*. Champaign, IL: Human Kinetics.

Buschner, C. (1994). *Teaching children movement concepts and skills: Becoming a master teacher*. Champaign, IL: Human Kinetics.

Carroll, M.E., & Garner, D.R. (1988). *Gymnastics 7-11: A lesson by lesson approach*. New York: Falmer Press.

Cooper, P.S., & Trnka, M. (1989). *Teaching basic gymnastics: A coeducational approach* (2nd ed.). New York: MacMillan.

Council on Physical Education for Children. (1992). *Developmentally appropriate physical education practices for children*. Reston, VA: National Association for Sport and Physical Education.

Franck, M., Graham, G., Lawson, H., Loughrey, T., Ritson, R., Sanborn, M., & Seefeldt, V. (1991). *Physical education outcomes: A project of the National Association for Sport and Physical Education*. Reston, VA: National Association for Sport and Physical Education.

Gerstung, S. (1974). *10 original tumbling charts*. Baltimore: Gerstung.

Graham, G. (1992). *Teaching children physical education: Becoming a master teacher*. Champaign, IL: Human Kinetics.

Graham, G., Holt/Hale, S., & Parker, M. (1993). *Children moving*. Mountain View, CA: Mayfield.

Hacker, P., Malmberg, E., Nance, J., Tilove, A., & True, S. (1993). *Sequential gymnastics for grades 3-6* (3rd ed.). Indianapolis: U.S. Gymnastics Federation.

Kelly, L.E. (1989). Instructional time: The overlooked factor in PE curriculum development. *Journal of Physical Education, Recreation and Dance*, **60**(6), 29-32.

Kirchner, G., Cunningham, J., & Warrell, E. (1978). *Introduction to movement education* (2nd ed.). Dubuque, IA: Brown.

Kruger, H., & Kruger, J. (1977). *Movement education in physical education*. Dubuque, IA: Brown.

Logsdon, B.J., Barrett, K., Broer, M., McGee, R., Ammons, M., Halverson, L., & Roberton, M. (1984). *Physical education for children*. Philadelphia: Lea and Febiger.

O'Quinn, G. (1978). *Developmental gymnastics*. Austin, TX: O'Quinn.

The Physical Education Association of Great Britain and Northern Ireland. (1991). Gymnastics—Ideals for the 1990's? *British Journal of Physical Education*, **22**(3), 8-35.

Purcell, T. (1994). *Teaching children dance: Becoming a master teacher*. Champaign, IL: Human Kinetics.

Ratliffe, T., & Ratliffe, L. (1994). *Teaching children fitness: Becoming a master teacher*. Champaign, IL: Human Kinetics.

Rink, J. (1993). *Teaching physical education for learning* (2nd ed.). St. Louis: C.V. Mosby.

Ryser, O., & Brown, J. (1990). *A manual for tumbling and apparatus stunts* (8th ed.). Dubuque, IA: Brown.

Shulman, L.S. (1987). Knowledge and teaching: Foundations of the new reform. *Harvard Educational Review*, **57**, 1-22.

Siedentop, D. (1991). *Developing teaching skills in physical education* (3rd ed.). Palo Alto, CA: Mayfield.

Stanley, S. (1977). *Physical education: A movement orientation* (2nd ed.). Toronto: McGraw Hill.

Williams, J. (1987). *Themes for educational gymnastics* (3rd ed.). London: Black.

Suggested Readings

Belka, D. (1993). Educational gymnastics: Recommendations for elementary physical education, *Teaching Elementary Physical Education*, **4**(2), 1-6.

This article compares educational gymnastics with Olympic gymnastics, pointing out how educational gymnastics is more appropriate in elementary school settings. It describes eight movement themes including weight bearing and weight transfer, dynamic and static balance, steplike movements, rocking and rolling, sliding, flight and landings, hanging and swinging, and climbing.

Carroll, M.E., & Garner, D.R. (1988). *Gymnastics 7-11: A lesson by lesson approach*. New York: Falmer Press.

This popular title views gymnastics from the perspective of education or body-management, providing primary teachers with practical assistance to structure meaningful lessons for young children. The lesson-by-lesson approach covers the 4-year period from 7 to 11 years. Specific skills are taught for regular use throughout the program.

Franck, M., Graham, G., Lawson, H., Loughrey, T., Ritson, R., Sanborn, M., & Seefeldt, V. (1991). *Physical education outcomes: A project of the National Association for Sport and Physical Education*. Reston, VA: National Association for Sport and Physical Education.

This project attempts to define the physically educated person, K to 12, in terms of the psychomotor, cognitive, and affective domains. Benchmarks for each grade level are described in such terms as *has* learned specific skills, *is* physically fit, *does* participate regularly, *knows* cognitive information, and *values* physical activity.

Graham, G. (1992). *Teaching children physical education: Becoming a master teacher*. Champaign, IL: Human Kinetics.

This text for the pedagogy course of the American Master Teacher Program for Children's Physical Education integrates research-based information with first-hand teaching experience. The book is an excellent resource for practical skills and techniques to help teachers motivate children to practice, build positive feelings, minimize off-task behavior and discipline problems, and create an atmosphere conducive to learning. It also develops lesson content and helps with problem solving, observation and analysis, feedback, and assessments.

Graham, G., Holt/Hale, S., & Parker, M. (1993). *Children moving*. Mountain View, CA: Mayfield.

This book develops skill themes that children can use as they move through levels of proficiency. The chapters on traveling, jumping and landing, rolling, balancing, and weight transfer are particularly appropriate for educational gymnastics.

Hacker, P., Malmberg, E., Nance, J., Tilove, A., & True, S. (1993). *Sequential gymnastics for grades 3-6* (3rd ed.). Indianapolis: U.S. Gymnastics Federation.

This book presents a guideline to establishing a safe, non-competitive environment in schools. Skill sequences require little or no spotting and are taught in progressive order, one skill building on another. Activities use mats, low balance beams, vault boards, and horizontal bars.

Human Kinetics. (in press). *Teaching for outcomes in elementary physical education: A guide for curriculum and assessment.* Human Kinetics: Champaign, IL.

This unique resource is divided into two parts. Part I introduces the concept of purposeful planning (creating curriculum goals or outcomes that are realistic and achievable for your particular situation) and then shows how to assess these goals using portfolio and performance task assessments. Teachers will find the many practical hints helpful, especially concerning the use and scoring of these assessments. Part II is organized according to the concepts (including fitness concepts) and skills taught in physical education and provides sample performance and portfolio tasks; teachers can use many of these to directly assess NASPE "Benchmarks," which are referenced when applicable. The "learnable pieces" are detailed for each skill and concept, along with activity ideas and practical hints for teaching them at the varying grade levels.

Kirchner, G., Cunningham, J., & Warrell, E. (1978). *Introduction to movement education* (2nd ed.). Dubuque, IA: Brown.

A fundamentally sound text, this book does not have separate chapters on games, dance, or gymnastics. Rather, it presents illustrated chapters on Laban themes of movement qualities (shape, direction, effort, and range) and the use of small and large apparatuses.

Kruger, H., & Kruger, J. (1977). *Movement education in physical education.* Dubuque, IA: Brown.

Taking a new look at physical education, attention is given to using 16 Laban themes. These fundamental themes serve as the basis for work in games, dance, and gymnastics.

Learmouth, J., & Whitaker, K. (1977). *Movement in practice.* Boston: Plays.

The authors present 14 educational gymnastics lessons. Each lesson includes a theme or combination of themes, an introductory exploratory phase, development of the theme through extensions and refinements, and the linking of the theme with apparatus work.

Mauldon, E., & Layson, J. (1979). *Teaching gymnastics* (2nd ed.). London: MacDonald and Evans.

Within a historical context the authors examine the relevance of gymnastics also in the context of the school curriculum. Based on educational gymnastics themes, the book serves the physical education specialist as well as the classroom teacher.

Morison, R. (1974). *A movement approach to educational gymnastics.* Boston: Plays.

The material in this book covers the full range of educational gymnastics for primary and secondary students. The actions emphasize locomotion and balance. Sub-themes for locomotion include transfer of weight, traveling, and flight. Sub-themes for balance include weight bearing, balancing skills, actions of arriving, and on- and off-balance actions. Partner and group work appear in a separate section.

O'Quinn, G. (1978). *Developmental gymnastics.* Austin, TX: O'Quinn.

This is a sequential model for Olympic gymnastics stunts, tumbling, and beginning apparatus work. Skills are presented in a developmental progression and illustrated well. Descriptions of the proper mechanics for each skill include important performance cues for execution. The book is oriented to beginners, ages 5 and 6, through the elementary years.

The Physical Education Association of Great Britain and Northern Ireland. (1991). Gymnastics—Ideals for the 1990's? *British Journal of Physical Education* **22**(3), 8-35.

This special issue presents the best of current theory and issues concerning educational gymnastics. It is a series of articles written by England's leading authorities on educational gymnastics.

Ravengo, I. (1988). The art of gymnastics: Creating sequences. *Journal of Physical Education, Recreation and Dance,* **59**(3), 66-69.

This article presents a clear outline of how to help children build sequences in gymnastics and includes several practical examples.

Rikard, G.L. (1992). Developmentally appropriate gymnastics for children. *Journal of Physical Education, Recreation and Dance*, **63**(6), 44-46.

Included in a special issue on developmentally appropriate physical education practices for children, this article gives many practical suggestions for teaching gymnastics. Rikard identifies inappropriate practices and suggests corrections.

Ryser, O., & Brown, J. (1990). *A manual for tumbling and apparatus stunts* (8th ed.). Dubuque, IA: Brown.

This guide is an excellent resource for physical education teachers on class organization and skill techniques in Olympic gymnastics. It also serves coaches of competitive gymnastics teams by providing competitive rules, background information, and skill progressions on the various competitive events.

Stanley, S. (1977). *Physical education: A movement orientation* (2nd ed.). Toronto: McGraw Hill.

Following the Laban movement framework, this book emphasizes the use of body awareness, space awareness, effort, and relationships in the teaching of games, dance, and gymnastics. The chapters on gymnastics offer selected lessons for children in the primary through the intermediate years.

Werner, P., & Sweeting, T. (1991). Gymnastics in schools. *The Physical Educator*, **48**(2), 86-92.

This article is based on the theoretical approach to modern educational gymnastics, which uses the themes of traveling, rotation, and static work as the foundation for gymnastics content. These themes are supported by the Laban process variables of body awareness, space awareness, effort actions, and relationships.

Williams, J. (1987). *Themes for educational gymnastics* (3rd ed.). London: Black.

This well-established book is a very useful, practical reference. Teachers can use its material as detailed lesson plans or as starting points.

About the Author

Peter Werner has more than 30 years' experience as a student and teacher of gymnastics. His background in Olympic and educational gymnastics provides him with an excellent developmental perspective to teaching gymnastics.

Peter earned his PED in physical education from Indiana University in 1971. He spent 6 months in 1987 at the University of Loughborough in England studying educational gymnastics. Peter teaches educational gymnastics and elementary physical education methods courses at the University of South Carolina, and he regularly spends time in the public schools teaching elementary physical education.

For 2 years Peter chaired the Southern District of the Council on Physical Education for Children (COPEC), and he was the publications coordinator for the National Association for Sport and Physical Education (NASPE) for 3 years. He has also written more than 40 articles and 5 books, including *Learning Through Movement*, and has made several national gymnastics presentations. Peter was selected the 1986 South Carolina Alliance of Health, Physical Education, Recreation and Dance College Teacher of the Year and was the recipient of the 1993 University of South Carolina Michael J. Mungo Teaching Award.

Peter is a member of the American Alliance of Health, Physical Education, Recreation and Dance, NASPE, and COPEC.

AMTP

American Master Teacher Program for Children's Physical Education

Learn practical strategies to help you improve children's physical education

The American Master Teacher Program (AMTP) curriculum consists of a Content Course, a Pedagogy Course, and the Master Teacher Practicum. All of these curriculum courses are taught by AMTP's National Faculty of outstanding elementary physical education specialists using state-of-the-art resources. By participating in AMTP you'll learn strategies, tecnniques, and skills for being an effective and enthusiastic physical education teacher—and receive recognition for achieving these goals. AMTP is a complete program designed to keep you on top of your profession by helping you

- bring your program in step with educational reform,
- network with your colleagues, and
- provide students with quality, developmentally appropriate physical education.

Pedagogy Course

The Pedagogy course focuses on "how to teach" and includes the following resources:

- *Teaching Children Physical Education: Becoming a Master Teacher*
- *AMTP Pedagogy Course Self-Study Video*
- *AMTP Pedagogy Course Study Guide*
- *AMTP Pedagogy Course Instructor Video*
- *AMTP Instructor Guide*

Content Course

This course examines "what to teach" and contains five books and companion videos:

- *Teaching Children Dance: Becoming a Master Teacher*
- *Teaching Children Fitness: Becoming a Master Teacher*
- *Teaching Children Games: Becoming a Master Teacher*
- *Teaching Children Gymnastics: Becoming a Master Teacher*
- *Teaching Children Movement Concepts and Skills: Becoming a Master Teacher*

Master Teacher Practicum

Once you have earned recognition as a Pedagogy and Content Specialist, you can apply for entry into the Master Teacher Practicum.

For additional information about AMTP courses and accompanying resources, contact

Linda Morford • P.O. Box 5076 • Champaign, IL 61825-5076 • TOLL-FREE 1-800-747-4457, ext 2258